AIR CAMPAIGN

YOM KIPPUR WAR 1973

Airpower in Israel's hardest-fought war

SHLOMO ALONI | ILLUSTRATED BY MADS BANGSØ

OSPREY PUBLISHING
Bloomsbury Publishing Plc
Kemp House, Chawley Park, Cumnor Hill, Oxford OX2 9PH, UK
29 Earlsfort Terrace, Dublin 2, Ireland
1385 Broadway, 5th Floor, New York, NY 10018, USA
E-mail: info@ospreypublishing.com
www.ospreypublishing.com

OSPREY is a trademark of Osprey Publishing Ltd

First published in Great Britain in 2024

A catalog record for this book is available from the British Library.

ISBN: PB 9781472858283; eBook 9781472858290
ePDF 9781472858269; XML 9781472858276

24 25 26 27 28 10 9 8 7 6 5 4 3 2 1

Maps by bounford.com
Diagrams by Adam Tooby
3D BEVs by Paul Kime
Index by Fionbar Lyons
Typeset by PDQ Digital Media Solutions, Bungay, UK
Printed and bound in India by Replika Press Private Ltd.

FSC
MIX
Paper from
responsible sources
FSC® C016779
www.fsc.org

Osprey Publishing supports the Woodland Trust, the UK's leading woodland
conservation charity.

To find out more about our authors and books visit www.ospreypublishing.com. Here
you will find extracts, author interviews, details of forthcoming events and the option to
sign up for our newsletter.

Photo on title page: see page 24.

Author's note
ILAF codes for radio call signs and for
operations are translated from Hebrew
to English.
ILAF names for aircraft and systems
are presented in English as they are
pronounced in Hebrew.
The events presented are based on
currently available primary sources
wherever possible.

Author's acknowledgements
Thanks to colleagues, family, friends,
organizations and veterans who have
supported the research that resulted in
this text.
Despite all best efforts, errors and
omissions are inevitable. Apologies.
Shlomo Aloni
25 January 2023

Times
All times presented are Israeli local times
which were, during the autumn of 1973,
two hours later than GMT, six hours
later than Washington, and the same
time for Egypt and Syria.

ABBREVIATIONS, ACRONYMS, CODES, and TERMS
AC: Author's collection
Ahit: ILAF Hebrew name for A-4 Skyhawk
Deker: ILAF Hebrew name for AIM-9D
Sidewinder
Egrof: ILAF Hebrew name for AGM-45
Shrike
FY: Fiscal Year
ILAF: Israel Air Force. In Israel, the IDF
chief of staff is the supreme commander
of the armed forces; the Israel Air Force
is an arm of the IDF and the ILAF
commander is subordinated to the IDF
chief of staff.
Kurnass: ILAF Hebrew name for F-4E
Phantom II
ILGD/A: Israel Government Defense/
Archive
ILGP/PO: Israel Government Premiere/
Press Office
Nesher: ILAF Hebrew name for IAI-
manufactured Mirage 5
PoW: Prisoner of War
QRA: Quick Reaction Alert
Saar: ILAF Hebrew name for J52-
powered Improved Super Mystère
SAM: Surface-to-Air Missile
Shahak: ILAF Hebrew name for Mirage
IIIC
Yasur: ILAF Hebrew name for Sikorsky
S-65/H-53 Stallion

CONTENTS

INTRODUCTION

The ILAF's greatest victory was accomplished during the June 1967 War, which started with Operation *Focus*, a knockout blow that generated images such as this photograph of a burning Egyptian Air Force Tu-16 bomber taken over Cairo West air base. Israeli expectations that the next war would start with another ILAF knockout did not turn into reality in the October 1973 War. (AC)

The October 1973 War is the most successful war in Israel's history. The prewar Israeli objective was the imposition of the Israeli government's territories-for-peace plan, to return Sinai to Egypt for nothing less than peace. In the wake of the October 1973 War, Egypt and Israel signed a peace treaty in 1979. Since the October 1973 War, Syria has been deterred and has not attacked Israel again.

Yet the Israeli military success in the October 1973 War was not as overwhelming as that of the June 1967 War. Israel won the June 1967 War by knockout in just six days, while the October 1973 War was a military victory on points, won over 19 days of fighting.

In addition, Israel's prewar military objective to win the war through the destruction of the enemy's military forces was not accomplished. The Israeli force that had been expected to generate this mass destruction of the enemy's military forces was the Israel Air Force (ILAF). Israel had been investing nearly 50 percent of its defense budget in the ILAF to create a force that would deter any enemy from starting a war and one which would destroy enemy military forces in a war if deterrence failed.

The ILAF had therefore failed on two counts: it didn't prevent the October 1973 War through deterrence and it didn't destroy the enemy's military forces. The centerpiece of the October 1973 conflict was the tank. After the war, Israel's Deputy Chief of Staff stated that the ILAF had destroyed less than 100 tanks during the war; years later a claim emerged that out of the 1,500 tanks examined postwar to ascertain cause of damage/destruction, not one was hit from the air. Likewise the ILAF's prewar plans to completely destroy the enemy's air forces and air defense forces had failed.

This book is the story of the ILAF's implementation of its prewar plans, its successes and failures, and how it contributed to an Israeli victory, militarily and diplomatically.

Background

The June 1967 Six Day War changed Middle East geopolitics. The presumed objective of the Egyptian-led Arab coalition – the destruction of Israel – was not accomplished. Israel

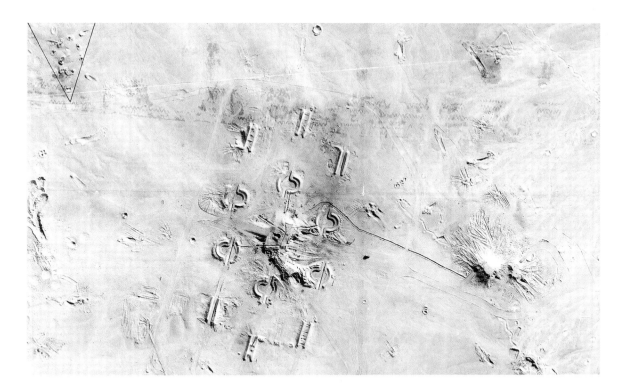

emerged victorious from the war and occupied territories larger than its own prewar size, gaining the Sinai Peninsula from Egypt, the West Bank from Jordan, and the Golan Heights from Syria.

The Israeli leadership during the conflict was the same leadership that had returned the strategically important Sinai region to Egypt in 1957 in exchange for US assurances to guarantee Israeli freedom of navigation through the Straits of Tiran at the southern tip of the Sinai Peninsula. The Egyptian blockade of Tiran and US hesitation in cashing in its commitments from 1957 resulted in the June 1967 War. Lessons had been learned and the same Israeli leadership that returned Sinai to Egypt in 1957 was adamant that the region would not be returned again for anything less than a peace treaty.

The Egyptian leadership was the same one that had repossessed Sinai in 1957 in exchange for minimal political payment as a result of international pressure placed upon Israel due to fears of creating a Cold War hotspot. Egypt was therefore eager to repossess Sinai again for minimal political payment – short of a peace agreement with Israel – through the creation of a regional hotspot that would motivate Cold War superpowers to force Israel to return the area to Egypt in order to cool the regional heat. Thus started more than a decade – from 1967 until 1979 – of a Middle Eastern clash of wills that would end back at its starting point.

That starting point was the Israeli government's territories-for-peace plan: Israel would return the Sinai Peninsula to Egypt – less the Gaza Strip – after the signing of a peace treaty with Egypt that would include (1) freedom of navigation through the Straits of Tiran, (2) freedom of navigation through the Suez Canal, (3) freedom of flight over Tiran, and (4) the demilitarization of Sinai.[1]

Egyptian SA-2 battery – actually an empty site – west of Fayid, west of Suez Canal Kilometer 107, photographed by an ILAF Shahak in December 1969. Egypt shifted defense of its front-line forces from the Egyptian Air Force to the Egyptian Air Defense in response to ILAF superiority in air-to-air warfare. The SA-2 battery comprises a command post surrounded by six launchers, with each rounded launch pad having an elongated trench for a replenishment missile. (AC)

1   The territories-for-peace plan as presented by the Israeli government meeting on June 19, 1967, was in essence the peace treaty that Egypt and Israel signed on March 26, 1979.

The Arab answer to the Israeli proposition was the "three nos" policy: no to recognition of Israel; no to negotiation with Israel; and no to peace. Egypt's President Nasser, whose slogan was "what has been taken by force will be returned by force," formulated a four-phase plan:

- Phase 1, "Firm Standing," during which Egypt would rebuild its armed forces that had been so heavily devastated during the June 1967 War.
- Phase 2, "Deterrence," during which Egypt would initiate low-scale fighting to erode Israel.
- Phase 3, "Elimination of [Israeli] Aggression [Accomplishments]," during which Egypt would regain control of territories lost during the June 1967 War, namely the Sinai Peninsula.
- Phase 4, "Final Victory."

As early as September 14, 1968, President Nasser announced progress from Phase 1 to Phase 2. Fighting between Egypt and Israel intensified to a limited war that earned its name, the War of Attrition, from Nasser's speech on June 23, 1969, when he stated: "I cannot invade Sinai but I can force attrition upon Israel to break its spirit."

Egypt's Phase 2 fighting created a regional hotspot, but Cold War geopolitics had by now changed. Egypt's ally, the USSR, was unable to force its will upon Israel without the cooperation of Israel's ally, the USA. The Egyptian blockade of the Straits of Tiran in 1967 did not only challenge Israel, but also challenged the USA's commitment to Israel; this time, the US government was willing to force Israel to return Sinai to Egypt only if the Israeli demands for peace were met.[2]

Israel feared that Egypt's creation of a regional hotspot still had the potential to cause international pressure for it to return Sinai to Egypt for something less than a peace deal. Moreover, the Egypt President's reference to breaking Israel's spirit touched a sensitive nerve in the Israeli mindset; it was feared that ongoing fighting with Egypt might result in internal political pressure to return Sinai to Egypt for something less than peace, perhaps for only a ceasefire agreement that would end hostilities for just a short while. Israel therefore worried that ongoing hostilities along the Suez Canal would result in international pressure or in internal weakness. Since Egypt was not willing to negotiate with Israel – the second section in its "three nos" policy – the only way for Israel to end hostilities along the Suez Canal was to escalate combat until Egypt accepted that fighting Israel was too costly to be continued. The Israeli Defense Minister, Moshe Dayan, labeled this policy "escalation to de-escalation."

Operation *Pomegranate*, launched in June 1969, was an Israeli air campaign aimed at shooting down Egyptian aircraft. ILAF fighters flew over Egypt seeking engagement

The Egyptian and Israeli air forces continued clashing occasionally between 1970 and 1973. This ILAF Squadron 201 Kurnass sight image captured the launch of an AIM-9D missile aimed at an Egyptian MiG-21 on June 13, 1972. The ILAF occasionally aspired to shooting down Egyptian and Syrian MiGs with the objective of deterring both nations from waging war against them through demonstration of the ILAF's superiority in air-to-air combat. (AC)

2   Peace between Egypt and Israel had been a US objective from at least 1955, and it was Egypt's rejection of the USA's proposition for economic aid conditioned upon peace with Israel that shifted Egypt to Soviet influence from 1955.

with Egyptian interceptors. *Pomegranate* resulted in the shooting down of several Egyptian aircraft, demonstrating ILAF superiority and sending Egypt a message that it should cease hostilities. Nevertheless, Egypt pursued fighting along the Suez Canal front line with artillery bombardments, sniper activity, and commando raids across the canal to ambush Israeli patrols.

Operation *Boxer* followed in July 1969, with Israel unleashing its air force against the Egyptian front line west of the Suez Canal. Although Egypt seemed to learn from *Pomegranate* and *Boxer* that the Egyptian Air Force was unable to protect its ground forces from the ILAF, fighting did not cease and Egyptian SAM batteries were deployed west of the Suez Canal to protect Egyptian troops from the ILAF. Israel responded with an air campaign against the SAM batteries west of the Suez Canal, and by the end of 1969, the ILAF had claimed the destruction of all SA-2 batteries west of the canal. With its ground forces fully exposed to the ILAF, Egypt continued fighting along the Suez Canal.

Operation *Blossom*, from January 1970, was the next Israeli escalation step aimed at de-escalating the War of Attrition to a ceasefire. ILAF Kurnass crews penetrated deep into Egypt and bombed Egyptian rear installations: barracks, depots, and training centers. The Israeli message to Egypt was that fighting along the Suez Canal could spread all over Egypt. As a democracy, the Israeli leadership feared that combat along the Suez Canal could erode the national resolve that Sinai should not be returned again for anything less than peace. As a dictatorship, the Egyptian leadership possibly feared that fighting all over Egypt might lead to internal unrest.

The USSR had backed the Egyptian leadership since 1955 through two major military defeats that had demonstrated the West's weapons superiority. With the East's prestige in danger, the USSR deployed an air defense division to Egypt to protect the interior of Egypt as well as to stabilize the nation's regime and to enable it to persist with fighting along the Suez Canal.

Israel called a halt to *Blossom* in April 1970 to avoid confrontation with the Soviet division that was defending Egypt's rear. The Israeli policy of "escalation to de-escalation" seemed to have reached a dead end, but the Soviets played into Israeli hands when they started rolling their integrated air defense system from Egypt's interior towards the Suez Canal front line. By the end of July 1970, Soviet SAMs had shot down five ILAF Kurnasses and Israeli pilots had shot down five Soviet MiG-21s. The clash between Israel and USSR was a draw, but the risk that the regional flames would evolve into a global fire was too great and Egypt was forced to accept a ceasefire from August 1970.

President Nasser's Phase 2 seemed to have failed. Israel now waited for the Egyptian President's next move, but it never came as Nasser died, aged only 52, on September 28, 1970.

Sadat succeeded Nasser and pursued his predecessor's policy, but warped Nasser's blunt rhetoric with his somewhat smoother initiative: Israel should withdraw east to enable the reopening of the Suez Canal, after which Israel should return Sinai to Egypt; only then would a diplomatic settlement be implemented.

Israel had been there before, returning Sinai to Egypt in 1957 for a lot less than peace, only to have to fight

ILAF commander Mordecai Hod, left, handed over command to Benjamin Peled, right, on May 10 1973. Hod had led the ILAF from 1966 through its greatest victory in Operation *Focus* and the June 1967 War, from the transition from French fighters to American aircraft, the emergence of the SAM threat over the front lines during the War of Attrition, and the expansion of the Israeli fighter force from some 200 aircraft in 1967 to nearly 400 by 1973. (ILGP/PO)

Egypt again in 1967. The Sadat initiative did not promise peace, and Israel was still unwilling to hand over its winning cards for anything other than that.

Sadat possibly realized that for as long as the USSR air defense division was deployed to Egypt, the Egyptian leadership would not be free to renew hostilities with Israel through progression from Nasser's Phase 2 to Phase 3. Sadat therefore expelled the Soviet unit from Egypt, but did not sever links with the USSR. Indeed, Soviet advisers remained in Egypt, and arms continued to flow into Egypt from the USSR. After the expulsion of the air defense division, Egypt was free to progress from Phase 2 to Phase 3, albeit a modified Phase 3.

Lessons that Egypt learned from the War of Attrition included that its air force was unable to protect its ground forces from the ILAF. Egypt's SAM force was therefore assigned that mission instead, but its engagement envelope ranged only up to 20km across the front line. Nasser's original Phase 3 had envisaged the invasion of Sinai, but the objective of the modified Phase 3 was to cross the Suez Canal and set foot in Sinai, with all crossing forces within the SAMs' engagement envelope. If Egypt's SAMs could crush the ILAF, then its air force would be able to protect the ground forces' advance deeper into Sinai. However, if the ILAF could not be defeated by the SAMs, then Egypt would still hold a narrow strip of land inside Sinai, east of the Suez Canal. Any resulting eventuality, from a limited Egyptian accomplishment to an overwhelming Egyptian victory, would hopefully lead to the repossession of Sinai from Israel for a payment short of peace.

The Egyptian Defense Force thus started planning and training for the modified Phase 3. Sadat set about forming a coalition against Israel, as Nasser had in 1967. Jordan and Syria were the obvious candidates to mesh with Egypt's modified Phase 3 plan. Jordan, however, had learned a harsh lesson from 1967 and did not join the new coalition. Syria did agree to attack Israel, though, so Israel would have to split its armed forces and simultaneously fight two wars with front lines some 500km apart: one along the Suez Canal in the south and another in the Golan Heights in the north. Sadat's Middle Eastern diplomatic offensive also resulted in Iraqi Hunter jets, Kuwaiti Lightnings, Libyan Mirages, Moroccan F-5s, and Saudi Lightnings being planned for deployment to Egypt.

The Iraqi Hunters and the Libyan Mirages were deployed to Egypt in April 1973. Israeli intelligence received information that Egypt would attack Israel around its 25th anniversary of Independence Day on May 7, 1973. Israel Defense Force units were initiated into a state of readiness labelled "Blue White": reserves were mobilized, front lines were bolstered, and plans were refreshed.

Nothing then happened; nothing except for massive damage to the shaky Israeli economy and some superficial cracks in the reputation of Israeli intelligence. Not only did Egypt not attack Israel in May 1973, but an Egyptian presidential adviser met his US counterpart to discuss the possible relaunch of the Egyptian plan for an Israeli retreat from Sinai, in what could have been anything from a sincere move to a smokescreen at a time when Israel was committed to a "territories-for-peace" plan and preparing for elections on October 30 of that year.

It was perfectly clear to all concerned that there would be no political progress prior to the Israeli elections. President Sadat did not wait for their outcome; on October 6, 1973, Egypt and Syria attacked Israel.

Three Wing 4 Khatsor-based Squadron 101 Shahaks lead and flank two of the first four F-4s to arrive in Israel on September 5, 1969. Israel purchased the F-4 as the new ILAF heavy attack aircraft. In 1967, the ILAF fielded only a single squadron with some 20 Vautour heavy attack aircraft out of around 200 combat aircraft; by 1973 it would possess four squadrons flying some 100 F-4 Kurnass heavy attack aircraft out of nearly 400 combat aircraft, emphasizing the ILAF's bias towards offense. (AC)

CHRONOLOGY

1967

June 10 The Six Day War ends in an Arab defeat and an Israeli victory. Israel occupies the Sinai Peninsula from Egypt, the West Bank from Jordan, and the Golan Heights from Syria.

June 19 Israeli government meeting confirms Israel's "territories-for-peace" plan.

September 1 The Khartoum Resolution is issued at the end of an Arab League summit in Sudan, under which there will be no peace with Israel, no recognition of Israel, and no negotiation with Israel.

1968

January 1 First flight of A-4 Ahits (Skyhawks) in Israel, the start of the ILAF transition from French fighters to American aircraft.

September 14 Egypt's President Nasser announces progress from Phase 1 to Phase 2; fighting between Egypt and Israel intensifies.

1969

June 24 Israel downs a MiG-21 over Egypt, the start of ILAF's Operation *Pomegranate* air campaign to down Egyptian Air Force fighters over Egypt.

July 20 ILAF's Operation *Boxer*, the start of ILAF bombings of Egyptian land forces west of the Suez Canal.

In 1971, the ILAF sponsored the production by the Israel Film Service and an Israel Defense Force spokesperson of the film *Mission Order 20*, which showed ILAF Kurnasses attacking a real former Egyptian SA-2 site in Sinai. This frame from the film clearly shows the large size of a SAM battery and the smaller size of the bomb's explosion, indicating that only a direct hit would result in destruction of any of a SAM battery's many components and only a near miss would inflict any damage. (AC)

September 5 ILAF accepts first four F-4 Kurnass aircraft from initial contract covering 50 to equip two new squadrons.

1970

January 7 ILAF Operation *Blossom 1* targets Egypt Air Defense SAM School and Egyptian Land Forces Special Forces Headquarters, the start of ILAF bombings of Egypt Defense Force rear installations in Egypt.

April 13 ILAF Operation *Blossom 21* ends ILAF bombings of Egypt Defense Force rear installations in an Israeli attempt to avoid confrontation with the USSR's air defense division that had been deployed to Egypt.

August 7 The War of Attrition between Egypt and Israel ends in a ceasefire, which was Israel's objective, while Egypt was probably forced to accept the ceasefire due to clashes between Israel and the Soviet air defense division.

September 28 Egypt's President Nasser surprisingly dies aged 52.

1971

February 5 Nasser's successor, President Sadat's initiative: Israel was to withdraw east so that the Suez Canal could be reopened, Israel to then withdraw from Sinai, and only after Sinai is returned to Egypt will a diplomatic settlement be negotiated. Israel rejects Sadat's initiative since it does not promise peace. The only path remaining for Egypt to regain Sinai for anything less than peace is a military action.

February 23 ILAF Exercise *Hit* – later to be referred to as *Hit 1* – simulates Operation *Challenge*, aimed at the destruction of Egypt Air Defense's front-line deployment of SAM batteries.

September 17 Egyptian SAMs launched across the Suez Canal down an ILAF C-97 flying a high-altitude oblique photography mission from north to south along the east bank of the Suez Canal, thus demonstrating the feasibility of Egypt Air Defense's potential to cover Egyptian land forces during crossing of the Suez Canal.

1972

July 17 The USSR air defense division starts its departure from Egypt, freeing Egypt to resume hostilities against Israel at will.

ILAF Squadron 107's Kurnass 175 returns to Wing 6 at Khatserim after air combat against Syrian MiG-21s on September 13, 1973. The Kurnass crew reported launching an AIM-9D missile at a MiG-21 but then breaking away, therefore not seeing the results, though another crew in their formation witnessed a hit. The ILAF credited the Kurnass 175 crew with one MiG-21 kill. (AC)

July 24 Egyptian SAM batteries west of the Suez Canal launch four or five missiles against two ILAF aircraft flying east of the Suez Canal, again demonstrating Egypt Air Defense's potential to cover Egyptian land forces during crossing of the Suez Canal.

October 18 ILAF Exercise *Hit 6* simulates Operation *Challenge*, aimed at the destruction of Egypt Air Defense front-line deployment of SAM batteries, and reveals a consistent 200m miss in Kurnass loft. Still, the ILAF concludes that attacking every SAM battery with three successive formations within a short timeframe will yield a destruction of 69 percent of the batteries after the first formation's attack, 87 percent after the second formation's attack, and 91 percent after the third formation's attack.

1973

February 25 Egypt presents a plan to the USA: Israel to return Sinai to Egypt until the end of 1973, with only then some sort of a diplomatic solution being implemented. The US response backs the Israeli proposition: first peace, then withdrawal.

March 1 US President Nixon meets Israeli Prime Minister Meir and reaffirms US commitment to back Israel's hard line, but somewhat surprisingly the Israeli Prime Minister does not reject the Egyptian plan and is seemingly willing to negotiate the reopening of the Suez Canal, possibly as a goodwill gesture. However, President Nixon asks Prime Minister Meir to avoid discussion of such potential concessions with the US State Department.

April 11 Israel receives intelligence information that Egypt will start a war against Israel in May 1973.

Israel Defense Force initiates "Blue White" readiness in preparation for war – including ILAF presentation of plans for war to the Israel Chief of Staff on April 25 and May 9 and then to Israel's Defense Minister on May 22 – but Egypt does not attack Israel that month and the Israel Defense Force ends "Blue White" on August 12, 1973.

August 25 The Egyptian and Syrian presidents meet to discuss plans for war against Israel. D-Day October 6, 1973, was reportedly agreed on September 12, with H-Hour set for 1400hrs as a compromise between Egypt's plan to attack from west to east at dusk and Syria's plan to attack from east to west at dawn.

September 13 Israeli and Syrian air forces clash in somewhat vague circumstances; the initial ILAF ambush seems to have gone awry even though the end result was an ILAF claim that 12 Syrian MiG-21s were shot down versus the loss of one Israeli Shahak.

September 25 Israel is informed that Syria is ready for imminent war against Israel, but Israeli intelligence treats the Syrian readiness as a repercussion of the September 13 clash. The analysis also states that Syria would not pursue war against Israel alone, without Egyptian participation, and that Egypt was preparing for a major military exercise that was only due to end on October 7.

October 6 Egypt and Syria attack Israel.

ATTACKER'S CAPABILITIES

The Egyptian Air Force fighter force was destroyed during the June 1967 War, but the majority of losses were on the ground, hence the number of pilots lost was a few dozen at most. Forward fields in Sinai were lost and several air bases west of the Suez Canal had to be abandoned, yet the Egyptian Air Force managed to quickly rehabilitate itself. The USSR supplied aircraft to replace losses and the Egyptians implemented lessons learned from the June 1967 War: shelters for aircraft, more runways, and fewer aircraft per air base. Within six years of the end of the June 1967 War, the Egyptian fighter force had been deployed to more than 15 air bases with at least two runways per base and shelters for most combat aircraft. An air superiority campaign to destroy the Egyptian Air Force within hours, like Israel's Operation *Focus* that opened the June 1967 War, was no longer a realistic option. The ILAF order of battle was too small for a simultaneous attack against all Egyptian air bases, while ILAF ordnance was inadequate for precision attacks aimed at the destruction of sheltered aircraft. Defensively, the Egyptian air force seemed to have gained an edge over the ILAF.

Offensively, however, the Egyptian Air Force faced a challenge. The loss of Sinai resulted in a longer distance from Egypt to Israel. Egyptian MiG and Sukhoi fighters lacked the range/load performances to attack Israel, while their Ilyushin and Tupolev bombers had the required range/load performances to go on the offensive but were relatively vulnerable. A combat aircraft in the F-4 class would have been ideal for the Egyptian air force, but Egypt's patron, the USSR, had no comparable machines. Egypt would seek long-range attack capability throughout the timeframe from 1967–73, but while some such capacity would be obtained, it was not enough to counter the formidable long-range heavy attack force that the ILAF would evolve over the same period. Egypt's air chiefs would have to tweak tactics to suit the available order of battle in light of the new reality.

Meanwhile, the Egyptian Air Force had to mesh with President Nasser's plan to repossess Sinai by force. Fighting the ILAF exposed Egypt's aerial weaknesses. Air-to-air combat revealed an ILAF advantage that also had an impact upon the Egyptian air force's air-to-ground operations. On top of the Egyptian Air Force's order of battle load and range issues, the

Egyptian MiG-17s reportedly photographed during an exercise in August 1972. The air forces of Egypt and Syria fielded seven MiG-17 squadrons with an estimated inventory of 240 aircraft, making the type the most prolific Egyptian and Syrian attack aircraft at the start of the October 1973 War. Algerian and Iraqi MiG-17s deployed to Egypt and Syria, respectively, after the start of the war. (AC)

OPPOSITE EGYPTIAN PREWAR DEPLOYMENT AND ORBAT

ILAF's air-to-air superiority forced the Egyptians to adopt hit-and-run tactics that minimized endurance across the front line. Israeli interceptors thus had less time to catch the intruders, thereby improving the survival rate of Egypt's attack aircraft, but as a result most Egyptian Air Force offensive operations during the War of Attrition were short-range missions.

The Egyptian armed forces internalized the country's aerial weaknesses and adjusted its plans accordingly. The modified Phase 3 plan suited the Egyptian Air Force perfectly; ground-based air defenses would defend the nation's ground forces along the front line, while the Egyptian Air Force would defend Egypt's rear. Egyptian Air Force offensive operations during the first phase of the planned fighting would be limited in range and scale so that its losses would be minimized. During that first phase of fighting, it would be mostly held back in a sort of reserve. Egypt expected that ILAF would respond with massive attacks against the Egyptian ground forces along the front line and deeper penetrations aimed at attacking Egypt's air bases. If ILAF close-support Ahit squadrons could be crushed by Egyptian air defense units over the front line and if Israel's heavy attack Kurnass force failed to destroy Egypt's major air bases, then the Egyptian Air Force could survive the first phase of fighting almost intact and consequently be able to cover the Egyptian ground forces during the war's second phase.

Israelis examining Egyptian MiG-17 wreckage – possibly number 2362 – in Tel Aviv in December 1967. (Israel National Library IPPA Dan Hadani Collection)

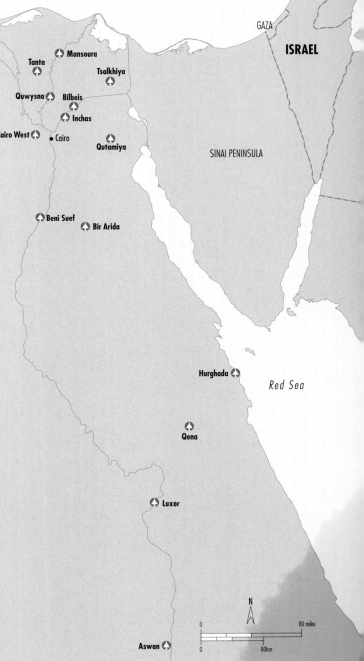

Mediterranean Sea

Tel Aviv •

GAZA

ISRAEL

Gianaclis

Tanta

Mansoura

Tsalkhiya

Quwysna Bilbeis

Inchas

Cairo West • Cairo

Qutamiya

SINAI PENINSULA

EGYPT

Beni Suef

Bir Arida

Hurghada *Red Sea*

Qena

Luxor

Aswan

N

0 ____ 80 miles

0 ____ 80km

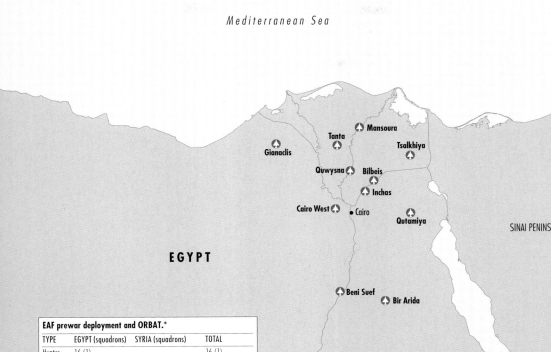

EAF prewar deployment and ORBAT.*			
TYPE	**EGYPT (squadrons)**	**SYRIA (squadrons)**	**TOTAL**
Hunter	16 (1)		16 (1)
Il-28	15		15
MiG-17	145 (3)	95 (4)	240 (7)
MiG-21	325 (12)	200 (8)	525 (20)
Mirage 5	17 (1)		17 (1)
Su-7	70 (3)	35 (2)	105 (5)
Su-17/20	27 (1)	15 (1)	42 (2)
Tu-16	25 (2)		25 (2)

* Nominal balance of power was roughly 1-to-2.5 since the ILAF estimated the combined enemy inventory of combat aircraft at 985:

Egypt*	Abu Khammad	1 MiG-21 squadron
	Aswan	1 Tu-16 squadron
	Beni Suef	1 MiG-21 squadron and 1 Su-20 squadron
	Bilbeis	3 Su-7 squadrons
	Bir Arida	1 MiG-21 squadron (North Korea)
	Cairo West	1 Tu-16 squadron
	Gianaclis	1 MiG-21 squadron and 1 Tu-16 squadron
	Hurghada	1 MiG-17 squadron
	Inchas	2 MiG-21 squadrons
	Luxor	1 MiG-21 squadron
	Mansura	2 MiG-21 squadrons
	Qena	1 MiG-21 squadron
	Qutamiya	1 MiG-17 squadron and 1 MiG-21 squadron
	Quwysna	1 Hunter squadron (Iraq)
	Shubra Khit	1 MiG-21 squadron
	Tanta	1 Mirage squadron
	Tsalkhiya	1 MiG-17 squadron

* Actual balance of power was 14 ILAF squadrons versus 38 squadrons based in Egypt and Syria on October 6, 1973.

Concurrent with planning and training, Egypt formed an alliance with Syria and assembled a coalition. Syria had also lost territory to Israel by the end of the June 1967 War, during which the ILAF had defeated the Syrian Air Force. The military lessons learned by Syria from the June 1967 War and subsequent clashes with Israel were generally similar to those of Egypt: shelters were needed for combat aircraft, along with additional air bases and eventually the deployment of Syrian SAM batteries to defend the Syrian ground forces along the front line. Syria's main objective was to repossess the Golan Heights, a strategically vital area smaller than the Sinai Peninsula, roughly 60km long and 30km wide. Most of the Golan Heights were within the Syrian SAM engagement envelope, while ILAF air bases and the interior of Israel were within range of Syrian combat aircraft. Nevertheless, Syria's strategy was similar to that of Egypt: its air defenses would defend the nation's ground forces along the front line, while its aerial forces conducted limited short-range offensive operations, defended Syria's rear, and would be held in reserve until the ILAF was crushed by the Syrian air defenses.

Egypt and Syria would be backed by a wider Arab coalition. Iraqi aircraft would deploy to Syria, while Algerian aircraft, Kuwaiti Lightnings, Libyan Mirages, Moroccan F-5s, and Saudi Lightnings would deploy to Egypt. Most of the planned deployments were to be implemented after the start of the war, but some were begun earlier in 1973 in advance of the planned war: an Egyptian MiG-17 squadron deployed to Syria, an Egyptian squadron flying Libyan Mirages moved from Libya to Egypt, an Iraqi Hunter unit deployed to Egypt, and a North Korean MiG-21 squadron deployed to Egypt.

The Egyptian and Syrian integrated air defense systems fielded some 180 SAM batteries, of which more than half were deployed with overlapping arcs of engagement to the west of the Suez Canal and to the east of the Golan Heights. SA-2 and SA-3 batteries were not mobile but could be redeployed between alternative sites. The SA-6 was a mobile system aimed at closing gaps in the coverage of the air defense system, able to deploy relatively quickly and with characteristics not yet known, meaning there were no electronic countermeasures against the SA-6. In addition, the SA-7 was a shoulder-launched short-range missile intended to augment antiaircraft artillery in the defense of targets under attack, with the added bonus that it could be quite easily deployed almost anywhere.

As well as the SAMs, two additional missile types were introduced to round off Egypt's preparations for war.

The AS-5 was an air-to-ground missile launched from Tu-16 bombers which homed in on sources of radiation, thereby transforming the Tu-16 from a penetrating bomber into a stand-off launch platform for precision attack against high-value assets: in particular, ILAF radar stations.

The other system, SCUD, was a ballistic missile with a 1,000kg warhead and a 300km range, but it lacked accuracy and a SCUD brigade could launch only some nine missiles in a salvo. Nevertheless, it helped make up for the Egyptian Air Force's lack of long-range attack capability and was primarily aimed at deterring Israel from tasking the ILAF to bomb targets in Egypt's rear.

A MiG-21 crossing the sights of an ILAF Shahak. The MiG-21 was the main Egyptian and Syrian combat aircraft at the start of the October 1973 War, with 20 squadrons and an estimated inventory of 525 aircraft, while more MiG-21s arrived in Egypt and Syria after the outbreak of hostilities: Algerian and Iraqi squadrons to Egypt and Syria, respectively, plus Soviet delivery of attrition replacement aircraft. (AC)

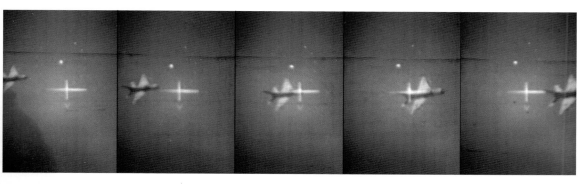

DEFENDER'S CAPABILITIES

The ILAF ended the June 1967 War with a remarkable exchange ratio of ten-to-one, but the 39 combat aircraft that it lost during the Six Day War represented almost 25 percent of its prewar order of battle. The Israel Defense Force's multi-year Maccabi Plan had previously aimed for an ILAF order of battle of 297 combat aircraft by March 31, 1970, as well as the construction of a sixth air base for combat aircraft. The downside of the Six Day War losses was that Israel would have to purchase additional combat aircraft to accomplish the Maccabi Plan objective for the ILAF's order of battle. The upside was that the ILAF order of battle mix would now include more modern combat aircraft than originally envisioned in Maccabi.

Maccabi was superseded by the Israel Defense Force's multi-year Goshen Plan, which envisaged 408 combat aircraft in the ILAF order of battle by March 31, 1973.[3]

However, existing French fighters flown by Israeli pilots were retired before the requisite number of American aircraft could be purchased, meaning that the ILAF order of battle on April 1, 1973, fell short of the Goshen objective, with just 357 combat aircraft.[4] . Nevertheless, the overall impact of the actual ILAF combat aircraft order of battle on April 1, 1973, was equal to or even more potent than that envisioned by the Goshen Plan.

By the time that Israeli intelligence expected Egypt to start a war in May 1973, the ILAF order of battle had undergone an impressive expansion in combat aircraft numbers and quality. Yet there were shortfalls in the ILAF's readiness for war. Some of the principal shortfalls were in weapons delivery systems, self-protection systems, and precision munitions.

The ILAF initiated the development of the Mirage 5 during the 1960s as a simplified fine-weather attack version of the all-weather Mirage IIIE interdictor. The ILAF actually misread

A Saar in a demonstration of ordnance options at Wing 4, Khatsor, in March 1973, from left to right: napalm, flares, rockets, Shafrir 2 for self-defense, fuel tank, and bombs. The ILAF order of battle included one Saar squadron primarily tasked to fly support missions. (AC)

---

3   Including 71 Kurnasses, 190 Ahits, and 15 Neshers, with the balance comprising the remaining French fighters: 43 Shahaks, 19 Saars, 14 Vautours, 21 Mystères, and 35 Ouragans.

4   100 Kurnasses, 33 Neshers, 36 Shahaks, 163 Ahits, and 25 Saars.

OPPOSITE ILAF PREWAR DEPLOYMENT AND ORBAT

the future, since by the 1970s a weapons delivery system was a must for an attack aircraft. The Nesher was a potent penetrator, but the lack of a weapons delivery system resulted in the assignment of the Neshers to augment the Shahaks as interceptors.

By the 1970s, SAM systems were the prime threat for Israeli combat aircraft in the Middle East, as they were for American aircraft operating over North Vietnam. The US Air Force equipped every combat aircraft tasked to operate over a SAM-defended zone with an electronic warfare pod for self-protection. However, the ILAF was somewhat skeptical concerning the efficiency of electronic warfare self-protection pods and acquired only a limited stock of older technology systems.

The ILAF had destroyed hundreds of aircraft and hundreds of vehicles with simple unguided weapons during the June 1967 War, using bombs, guns, and rockets. By 1973, shelters protected aircraft and SAMs protected targets on the battlefield. Guns were no longer relevant for the destruction of aircraft on the ground. Closing in for bombing, gunnery, and rocketry attacks in order to destroy targets on the battlefield became much more risky. What was needed in 1973 to destroy an aircraft on the ground was a weapon accurate enough to hit a shelter and heavy enough to penetrate that shelter. To hit a tank on the battlefield, an accurate weapon was required that could be released outside the engagement envelope of the protecting SAM systems, or the SAM systems had to be destroyed first before hitting the tanks from close range. The ILAF inventory included small numbers of precision munitions – GBU-8s, AGM-12s, and AGM-62s – but none ideally suited to operations against well-defended shelters and tanks, while none had a longer engagement range than that of the defending SAMs. Bombs and rockets remained the ILAF's principal offensive weapons.

There were three main ILAF attack profiles. Dive bombing was the simplest and most accurate attack profile, but it was not safe against targets within SAM-defended zones. For attack missions within SAM-defended zones, the Israelis avoided the US Air Force's pod formation that bombed from medium altitude, with each aircraft's self-protection pod providing a part in the combined overall protection for the attackers. The ILAF did not have enough self-protection pods, regarding the US Air Force's pod formation tactic as too risky and overall seeming to have little faith in intangible, unseen electronic wizardry. Instead, the ILAF's preferred profiles for attacking targets within SAM-defended zones were what was known as loft and pop.

In both loft and pop, the attacking aircraft approached the target flying fast and low. Their speed provided protection against antiaircraft fire and SA-7 missiles, while flying at low altitudes delayed detection by surveillance radars and minimized the available timeframe for lock-on by SAM fire control radars.

An Ahit H – ILAF parlance for the A-4H – displaying the ordnance of the ILAF light attack aircraft at Air Base 8 Ekron in April 1970. By October 1973, the ILAF fielded seven Skyhawk squadrons, of which five were operational: one Ahit N squadron, two Ahit H squadrons, and two Ahit E squadrons. (AC)

In loft, the pilot pulled up several kilometers short of the target, released the bombs while climbing so that the bombs would ascend and drop straight ahead in a ballistic trajectory, meanwhile the attacking aircraft turned back and dived to the deck, avoiding flying over the SAM-defended target but nevertheless still penetrating the outer edge of the SAM zone as loft delivery range was shorter than that of the SAMs. Loft was obviously not a precision attack profile, but a sort of area bombing. In the absence of better solutions, loft was a viable attack profile either as a nuisance to harder front-line targets with

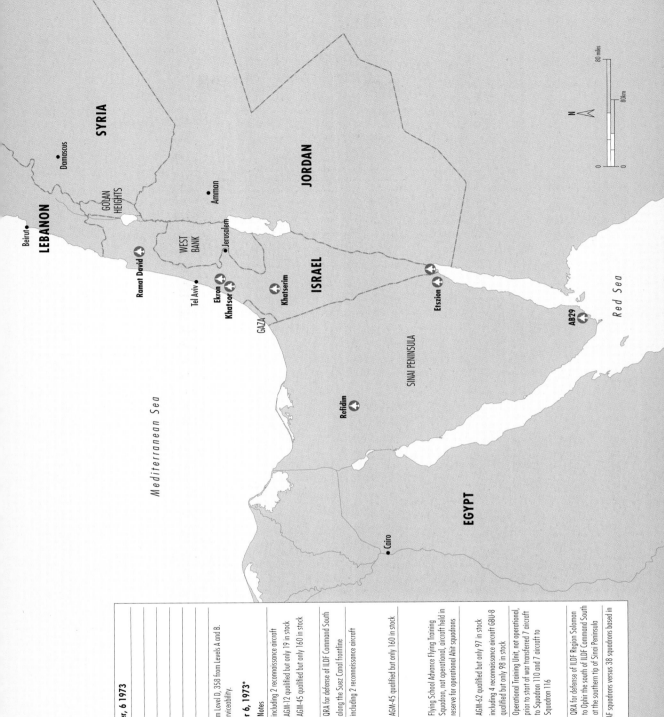

ILAF prewar deployment and ORBAT October, 6 1973

Type	Total	Level D
Kurnass	109	2
Ahit	181	19
Shahak/Nesher	76	7
Saar	25	5
TOTAL	391*	

*Includes eight unarmed reconnaissance aircraft, 33 from Level D, 358 from Levels A and B. Levels A and B were available to squadrons with 85% serviceability.

Deployment of ILAF combat aircraft: October 6, 1973*

Base/wing	Squadron	A+b	D	Notes
Wing 1	69 Kurnass	29	1	including 2 reconnaissance aircraft
Ramat David	109 Ahit H	30	3	AGM-12 qualified but only 19 in stock
	110 Ahit E	25	7	AGM-45 qualified but only 160 in stock
	117 Shahak	16	3	
Air Base 3	101 Shahak	2	-	QRA for defense of ILDF Command South along the Suez Canal frontline
Refidim	119 Kurnass	2	-	
Wing 4	101 Shahak/Nesher	15	2	including 2 reconnaissance aircraft
Khatsor	105 Saar	20	5	
	113 Nesher	18	1	
	201 Kurnass	25	1	AGM-45 qualified but only 160 in stock
Wing 6	102 Ahit H	29	2	
Khatserim	107 Kurnass	24		
	147 Ahit T	22	1	Flying School Advance Training Squadron, not operational, aircraft held in reserve for operational Ahit squadrons
Air Base 8	115 Ahit N	25	2	
Ekron	116 Ahit E	17	4	AGM-62 qualified but only 97 in stock
	119 Kurnass	27		including 4 reconnaissance aircraft GBU-8 qualified but only 98 in stock
Wing 10	140 Ahit E	14		Operational Training Unit, not operational, prior to start of war transferred 7 aircraft to Squadron 110 and 7 aircraft to Squadron 116
Etszion				
Air Base 29	144 Nesher	18		
	107 Kurnass	2		QRA for defense of ILDF Region Solomon to Ophir the south of ILDF Command South at the southern tip of Sinai Peninsula

* Actual balance of power in combat aircraft was 14 ILAF squadrons versus 38 squadrons based in Egypt and in Syria.

iron bombs or more effectively against softer second-line targets with cluster bombs, though obviously second-line softer targets mattered less to the war's outcome than harder targets in the front line.[5]

In pop, the pilot approached the target at low altitude, popped up quickly over a predefined point short of the target to get a glimpse of the target area, then immediately dived to bomb, thus minimizing the exposure timeframe to antiaircraft fire and SAM launches. Pop was the Israelis' preferred pattern for attacking SAM-defended large targets in the rear of enemy territory: air bases, command posts, communication centers, and radar stations. Pilots flying pop could not avoid overflying the target, meaning that while more accurate than loft, it was also riskier.

Order of battle, weapons, and tactics were embedded in the preparation of contingency plans:

Scratch was the ILAF's reaction to a surprise offensive against Israel. The Israel Defense Force pinpointed potential crossing points along the Suez Canal and penetration paths in the Golan Heights. In a *Scratch* scenario, the ILAF's initial reaction would be to harass the enemy's crossing points and penetration paths. Flying loft and pop profiles within SAM-defended zones against predesignated targets was not expected to yield accurate hits, but showering cluster bombs against crossing points and penetration paths could cause some slowing of the flow of enemy forces that were superior in numbers to regular Israeli ground forces holding the lines. Only prior to – or even after – the arrival at the front lines of Israel Defense Force reserves, within 24–72 hours or so, would the ILAF activate air superiority plans in order to support counteroffensives by Israeli forces.

Challenge was an air superiority plan aimed at destroying Egyptian SAM batteries west of the Suez Canal prior to the start of an Israeli offensive, either in an Israeli preplanned war or prior to the start of an Israeli counteroffensive in a *Scratch* scenario. Destruction of the Egyptian air defenses was aimed at enabling Israel to fly dive-bombing mission profiles over the front lines to improve target acquisition and bombing accuracy, as well as enabling attack aircraft to drop guided munitions.

Challenge seems to have been an ILAF frontal charge against Egypt's SAM batteries all along the 160km of the Suez Canal. There seems to have been no mesh between the ILAF's *Challenge* and Israel Defense Force's Command South offensive plans, each of which targeted a certain sector of the Suez Canal. Since Israeli air superiority campaigns were primarily intended to precede Israel Defense Force offensives rather than being a stand-alone action, there seems to have been a flaw in the plan to accomplish air superiority all along the Suez Canal prior to a Command South offensive at a certain sector of the front line.[6]

5   The ILAF Hebrew term for the loft profile was *kela*. Kurnass crews related the profile to the English term "loft" probably because the F-4's computer mode for that profile was LOFT and an ILAF modification to that mode was termed LOFT TOSS. Ahit pilots related the profile to the English term "toss". The term "loft" is used in this text.

6   The Israel Defense Force's Branch General Department Operations Chief raised the question of *Challenge*'s link with Command South's actual operations during presentation of ILAF plans to the IDF on April 25, 1973. The ILAF stressed that it was not worthwhile for *Challenge* to destroy only SAM sites essential to enabling Command South operations in a particular sector; it was intended to suppress all SAM batteries across the front line. The ILAF also stressed that *Challenge* was aimed at preceding a Command South offensive across the Suez Canal. If *Challenge* was not followed by a Command South armored advance, then Egypt would be able to rehabilitate its front-line SAM batteries within 24 hours for hasty positioning of some SAM batteries and within 48 hours for proper positioning of the integrated air defense system.

Model was an air superiority plan aimed at destroying Syrian air defense deployment of SAM batteries east of the Golan Heights. The length of the Golan Heights front line was less than a third of that of the Suez Canal and the number of Syrian SAM batteries east of the Golan Heights was also roughly a third of the number of Egyptian SAM batteries west of the Suez Canal, so *Model* was planned to challenge the Syrian Air Defense deployment east of the Golan Heights in a single wave.

Ram was a series of contingency plans aimed at attacking enemy air bases. The plans ranged from an attack against a single air base to a combined operation against the Egyptian or Syrian air forces.

The objective of each raid was defined as suppression or destruction. Suppression was intended to close an air base for operations for several hours or days, whereas destruction was defined as rendering an air base unfit for operations for the duration of a war. Egyptian and Syrian bases changed between 1967 and 1973. There were more Egyptian and Syrian air bases in 1973, and these had been hardened with shelters for aircraft. The ILAF's air base attack tactics also changed. In 1967, small formations attacked an air base successively, each formation flying several passes during a 15-minute timeframe so that an air base was under attack for several hours, the Israeli objective being to destroy aircraft. By 1973, however, the ILAF's tactics had switched to a massive hit-and-run attack on a base. A small vanguard would loft cluster bombs to overwhelm the air base defenses, then the main attack force would follow within a minute, flying pop at a rate of up to eight attacking aircraft per minute, each dropping up to ten bombs. For suppression, the main force would include less than ten attacking aircraft and the main targets would be the base's runways. For destruction, the main force would include some 50 attacking aircraft and the top targets would be shelters. A suppression attack on an enemy air base would last less than five minutes, while a destruction attack would continue for less than ten minutes. Unable to cover all of air bases in Egypt or Syria in a single wave or even in a single day, the ILAF could knock out bases one after the other only if the objectives of destruction and suppression had been accomplished. There was one principal flaw in *Ram*, and many more problems would surface when *Ram* was implemented. The major problem was regarding precision and penetration. The ILAF depended on statistics for precision, dropping hundreds of bombs over an air base with dozens of shelters, hoping that each shelter would be hit by at least one bomb and figuring that a direct hit by a 750lb M117 bomb would destroy a shelter along with the aircraft within it. In the event of war, the Israeli aerial and ground forces would have to prioritize between *Challenge*, *Model*, and *Ram*. Prioritization was also an element of *Ram*. Aiming at air superiority and neglecting the threat posed to Israeli ground forces by Egyptian attack aircraft, the ILAF prioritized for *Ram* Egypt's MiG-21 bases.

Dominique and *Plow* were plans to bomb rear targets deeper inside Egypt and Syria in a bid to indirectly influence the course of the war. *Dominique*'s targets were mostly electricity, headquarters, POL (petrol, oils, lubricants), and transport infrastructure, while *Plow*'s targets were communication centers.

Neshers – Mirage 5s assembled in Israel – were originally purchased by the ILAF with the intention of service as an interdictor, but the shift from French fighters to American aircraft and the Nesher's lack of systems comparable to the avionics in the Ahit and Kurnass resulted in an almost exclusive assignment of Neshers to air-to-air missions, regardless of this seemingly potent air-to-ground configuration on display at Wing 4, Khatsor, in March 1973 with seven bombs, two fuel tanks, and two Shafrir 2 air-to-air missiles. (AC)

CAMPAIGN OBJECTIVES

Israel unveiled the indigenous Rafael Shafrir 2 air-to-air missile on March 27, 1973 – ahead of the 25th Israel Independence Day on May 7 – at a time when the missile had been in service since 1969 and had already been credited with air-to-air kills. The ILAF's inventory on October 6, 1973 would include 293 Shafrir 2 missiles, as well as 148 AIM-7s and 642 AIM-9B/D/G air-to-air missiles. (ILGP/PO)

Egypt's objective was to set foot in Sinai through occupation of a narrow strip of land east of the Suez Canal and within the engagement envelope of its SAM batteries deployed along the west bank of the canal. If Egyptian Air Defense SAM batteries could erode the ILAF order of battle, then Egyptian land forces would launch a second-wave offensive to advance deeper into Sinai. Either way, end-of-war Egyptian objectives were the reopening of the Suez Canal as a direct result of the military action, and the generation of international political pressure that would force Israel to return the Sinai Peninsula to Egypt for an Egyptian political payment short of peace.

Syria's objectives were to retake the Golan Heights and Mount Hermon, which had been lost to Israel in the June 1967 War. Mount Hermon was an isolated fort on top of a 2,000m-high mountain, while the compact size of the Golan Heights – which was significantly smaller than the Sinai Peninsula – meant it could potentially be occupied in a single attack run from east to west, ending along the western side of the Golan Heights, the pre-June 1967 War border line.

Israel's objective was to win the war through destruction of Egyptian and Syrian military power, hopefully without the loss of territory and preferably without gaining ground, since the front lines achieved by the June 1967 War in both the north and south were the shortest for defense of the Golan Heights and Sinai Peninsula. The line from Mount Hermon to Canyon Ruqad in the north and the Suez Canal in the south were the shortest possible geographic lines for the defense of these two areas.

Orders of battle

Israel faced a war against a coalition led by Egypt and Syria, with a prewar preparation timeframe of less than 24 hours. The prewar timeframe that preceded the June 1967 War had lasted three weeks, enabling the ILAF to return to service aircraft with depot-level maintenance in order to achieve 97 percent serviceability in combat aircraft in its order of battle. The much shorter prewar timeframe in 1973 resulted in Israel's inability to accomplish a higher than normal combat aircraft serviceability for the crucial Day 1 of the looming clash. The ILAF combat aircraft order of battle on October 6, 1973, was as follows:

Type	Total	Level D	Notes
Kurnass	109	2	including 6 reconnaissance aircraft
Ahit	181	19	
Shahak/Nesher	76	7	including 2 reconnaissance aircraft
Saar	25	5	

The number of Israeli combat aircraft on October 6, 1973, was therefore 391, including eight unarmed reconnaissance aircraft, of which 33 were in Level D (undergoing major maintenance or being rebuilt in depots) and 358 were in Levels A (available in squadrons) and B (undergoing inspections and repairs in maintenance squadrons). Aircraft in Levels A and B were available to the squadrons with 85 percent serviceability on October 6, 1973. The deployment of ILAF combat aircraft on October 6, 1973, was as follows:

Base/wing	Squadron	A+B	D	Notes
1st Wing	69 Kurnass	29	1	including two reconnaissance aircraft
Ramat David	109 Ahit H	30	3	AGM-12 qualified but only 19 in stock
	110 Ahit E	25	7	AGM-45 qualified but only 160 in stock
	117 Shahak	16	3	
Air Base 3	101 Shahak	17	2	QRA for defense of Command South
Refidim	119 Kurnass	29	2	along the Suez Canal front line
4th Wing	101 Shahak/ Nesher	17	2	including two reconnaissance aircraft
Khatsor	105 Saar	20	5	
	113 Nesher	18	1	
	201 Kurnass	25	1	AGM-45 qualified but only 160 in stock
6th Wing	102 Ahit H	29	2	
Khatserim	107 Kurnass	24		
	147 Ahit T	22	1	Flying School Advance Flying Training Squadron, not operational, aircraft held in reserve for operational Ahit squadrons
Air Base 8	115 Ahit N	25	2	
Ekron	116 Ahit E	17	4	AGM-62 qualified but only 97 in stock
	119 Kurnass	29		including four reconnaissance aircraft GBU-8 qualified but only 98 in stock
10th Wing	140 Ahit E	14		Operational Training Unit, not operational
Etszion				prior to start of war transferred seven aircraft to Squadron 110 and seven aircraft to Squadron 116
	144 Nesher	18	1	
Air Base 29	107 Kurnass	24		QRA for defense of Region Solomon to Ophir the south of Command South at the southern tip of Sinai Peninsula

The ILAF's actual front-line force therefore included four Kurnass squadrons, five Ahit squadrons, four Nesher/Shahak squadrons, and one Saar squadron.

The nominal balance of power in combat aircraft was roughly 2.5-to-1 in favor of their opponents, as the ILAF estimated a combined enemy inventory of 985 combat aircraft, as follows:

Type	Egypt (squadrons)	Syria (squadrons)	Total
Hunter	16 (1)		16 (1)
Il-28	15		15
MiG-17	145 (3)	95 (4)	240 (7)
MiG-21	325 (12)	200 (8)	525 (20)
Mirage 5	17 (1)		17 (1)
Su-7	70 (3)	35 (2)	105 (5)
Su-17/20	27 (1)	15 (1)	42 (2)
Tu-16	25 (2)		25 (2)

The actual balance of power in combat aircraft was 14 ILAF squadrons versus 38 squadrons based in Egypt and in Syria on October 6, 1973:

Egypt	
Abu Hammad	1 MiG-21 squadron (Squadron 82)
Aswan	1 Tu-16 squadron
Beni Suef	1 MiG-21 squadron, 1 Su-20 squadron
Bilbeis	3 Su-7 squadrons
Bir Arida	1 MiG-21 squadron (North Korea)
Cairo West	1 Tu-16 squadron
Gianaclis	1 MiG-21 squadron, 1 Tu-16 squadron
Hurghada	1 MiG-17 squadron
Inchas	2 MiG-21 squadrons
Luxor	1 MiG-21 squadron
Mansura	2 MiG-21 squadrons
Qena	1 MiG-21 squadron
Qutamiya	1 MiG-17 squadron, 1 MiG-21 squadron
Quwaysna	1 Hunter squadron (Iraq)
Shubra Khit	1 MiG-21 squadron
Tanta	1 Mirage squadron
Tsalkhiya	1 MiG-17 squadron
Syria	
Baly	1 MiG-17 squadron
Dumayr	2 MiG-21 squadrons
Khalkhala	1 MiG-21 squadron
Khamat	1 MiG-21 squadron
Mazzeh	3 MiG-17 squadrons, including 1 Egyptian
Nassariya	1 MiG-21 squadron
Nayrab	1 MiG-21 squadron
Qutsayr	1 MiG-21 squadron
Syqal	1 MiG-21 squadron
T-4	2 Su-7 squadrons, 1 Su-20 squadron

The ILAF's standard for a combat aircraft squadron was 24 aircraft, while it estimated that the standard for a combat aircraft squadron in Egypt and Syria was around 20 aircraft. The actual balance of power in front-line combat aircraft on October 6, 1973, was therefore 336 ILAF versus up to 760 Egyptian and Syrian air force.

An Israeli Defense Force Tiran tank commander – a lieutenant colonel – salutes Israeli chief of staff Elazar, Prime Minister Meir, President Shazar, Defense Minister Dayan, and Israel Defense Force command center chief Zeevi during the Israel Independence Day 25 parade in Jerusalem on May 7, 1973. The Tiran was a T-54/T-55 tank captured in the June 1967 War and modified with Israeli Defense Force armor, communication systems, and weapon systems – a 105mm cannon and Browning machine gun. (ILGP/PO)

Although the balance of power in combat aircraft was not on a par, the ILAF had narrowed the gap in quantity and held the edge in quality. The F-4 and MiG-21, as well as the A-4 and MiG-17, had similar aerodynamic performances, yet the Ahit and Kurnass were superior in load, range, and systems. Israel's smaller number of combat aircraft could lift a combined total offensive load heavier than the larger number of Egyptian and Syrian combat aircraft, over longer ranges, and more accurately. This highlighted the fact that the ILAF was primarily an offensive force.

To counter the ILAF's offensive plans, Egypt and Syria fielded integrated air defense systems that according to the ILAF included the following:

Type	Egypt	Syria
SA-2	76 batteries, including 35 along front line	13, including 7 along front line
SA-3	64 batteries, including 20 along front line	8, including 3 along front line
SA-6	10 batteries, all along front line	15, all along front line

Egypt and Syria would be the offensive side at the start of the coming war, but the Egyptian and Syrian air forces and air defenses were more defensive than offensive, primarily to suit Egyptian and Syrian expectations that Israel would not remain on the defensive for long. Egyptian and Syrian plans were to attack in order to gain ground, but then to defend the gained ground in the face of Israel's counteroffensives. The attacking nations' air orders of battle were thus more defensive than offensive, while the air order of battle of the country to be attacked was much more offensive than defensive.

THE CAMPAIGN

The scene at the ILAF's Wing 4, Khatsor, at around 1100hrs on October 7, with Squadron 105 Saars taxiing to takeoff and Squadron 201 Kurnasses preparing to depart for Operation *Model 5* missions. (AC)

Egypt and Syria attacked Israel at 1400hrs on October 6, 1973. Five Egyptian divisions started crossing the Suez Canal to set foot in the Sinai Peninsula along the east bank of the waterway. Three Syrian divisions meanwhile began advancing towards the Golan Heights through penetration paths.

Israel was not surprised. A warning that war would start on October 6 was acknowledged in Israel at around dawn that same morning. Mobilization of Israel Defense Force reserves started on the morning of October 6, several hours before the start of the war, but these forces were not expected to arrive at the front lines within less than 24–72 hours. The smaller Israeli regular force would have to defend the Golan Heights and the Sinai Peninsula until the arrival at the front lines of the nation's larger reserve force.

The principal Israel Defense Force fighting tool was the tank, with some 300 in the south and just short of 200 in the north. The balance of power in tanks was no more than three-to-one against the Israelis. The ILAF's activation of *Scratch* would enable the regular Israeli ground forces, with massive loft and pop air support against crossing points in the south and penetration paths in the north, to hold their lines. Then the organized and fresh Israeli reserve forces would arrive at the front lines to initiate counteroffensives that could destroy enemy forces and win the war for Israel.

The advance notice of war was somewhat counterproductive for both the Israel Defense Force and the ILAF, because Israel was led to believe – probably deceived to believe – that H-Hour would be at dusk, around 1800hrs. It was only four hours past the actual H-Hour of 1400hrs, but it made a huge difference.

The Command South routine deployment was one armored brigade along the front line and two armored brigades held back. Command South's plan to defend the Suez Canal line was to deploy two armored brigades forward with a third armored brigade held back for reinforcements and counterattacks. Expecting war to start at 1800hrs, Command South did not rush with the deployment forward of the second armored brigade. When Egyptian infantry started crossing the Suez Canal, the Command South tanks were moved rapidly forward, only to be caught in the open by Egyptian tanks firing from ramps along the west bank of the Suez Canal and Egyptian infantry antitank weapons positioned on Israeli tank ramps east of the Suez Canal that had been empty and hence easily occupied by the crossing Egyptian infantry. By the end of the day, Command South had lost two-thirds of its tanks and the Egyptian crossing of the Suez Canal had positioned five divisions along a narrow strip of land east of the canal, having suffered relatively light losses.

The Command North Chief was visiting the Chief of Staff in Tel Aviv at the time the war started. Two of his armored brigades defended the Golan Heights: Brigade 7, with three battalions in the north sector of the Golan Heights; and Brigade 188, with two battalions in the south sector of the Golan Heights. The commander of Brigade 188 was acting Command North chief at its forward command post behind the lines of Brigade 7. By the time the Command North chief arrived to relieve the Brigade 188 commander, Brigade 7's battalions were holding the line in the north sector of the Golan Heights but Syrian armor had penetrated the south sector's first line of defense and started to advance west over the flatter terrain of this part of the Golan Heights. To the north of Brigade 7's sector, Syrian Mi-8 helicopters landed a commando force close to Israel's Mount Hermon fort at around 1500hrs. Within hours, the Syrian commandos captured the fort, thereby denying Command North an observation post from where the whole Golan Heights was visible, as well as the areas to the rear of the front line and east towards Damascus, a position that could have been vital for ILAF air superiority offensive planners.

The ILAF was not surprised either. If war had started without Israel receiving intelligence of an impending attack, then it would have activated *Scratch*. Within minutes of the activation of *Scratch*, Israeli attack aircraft would have mounted loft and pop operations against Egyptian crossing points and Syrian penetration paths. Showering cluster bombs

A view from space – taken by NASA in October 1968 – illustrates the Israeli problem on October 6, 1973 when faced with fighting two simultaneous wars with front lines some 500km apart, with the ILAF as the only Israeli High Command force able to support either front at short notice. For major ILAF offensives, Syria had been prioritized over Egypt because the Sinai Peninsula was a large buffer zone between the front line and Israel, while the Syrian Air Force was prioritized over the Syrian Air Defense because Syria's combat aircraft were much closer and able to attack within Israel. Attacking Syrian air defense units was to follow the ILAF's offensive against the Syrian Air Force and precede a Command North counteroffensive. (NARA)

OPPOSITE EGYPTIAN WAR PLANS

President Nasser's Phase 3 war was aimed at recapturing the whole Sinai Peninsula. Sadat's Phase 3 war aimed to set foot in Sinai and was divided into two phases, as presented over a contemporary ILAF map:
Stage 1 was the crossing of the Suez Canal by five infantry divisions, with bridgeheads within range of Egyptian Air Defense SAM battery engagement arcs.
Stage 2 was an advance deeper into Sinai to be spearheaded by Armored Division 4, Armored Division 21, and Armored Brigade 25, not to recapture the whole of Sinai but with more modest objectives.
Stage 2 was dependent upon the crushing of the ILAF by the Egyptian air defenses, the repelling of the expected Command South counteroffensive, and the preservation of the Egyptian Air Force, because air defense elements protected Egyptian forces during Stage 1 and aerial units were planned to support them during Stage 2.
The map clearly shows that the Suez Canal is the shortest line between Egypt and Sinai. Any Egyptian advance east beyond the range of their air defense deployment along the Suez Canal would have resulted in longer lines, so even the forwarding of SAM batteries would have resulted in diluted coverage, hence the importance for the Egyptian Air Force of an Egyptian Stage 2 offensive.

over these areas may not have stopped the push forward by the Egyptian infantry and Syrian armor, but would surely have had some sort of an impact, bearing in mind the Israeli objective to win the war through the destruction of enemy forces.

Israel was not surprised, and *Scratch* was not activated. Moreover, Israel had been led – or misled – to believe that war would start at dusk, and *Scratch* was far less effective during nighttime. Politically, preemptive action *à la* June 1967's Operation *Focus* was not an option in 1973, as Israel was not willing to start a war. Nevertheless, with prior notice that war would start at dusk, the offensive-minded ILAF went to the Israel Defense Force with a plan for a preemptive offensive against Syria, at first planning to implement Operation *Model* against Syrian SAM batteries from 1100hrs before switching to Operation *Ram* against Syrian air bases from 1200hrs.[7]

Why did the ILAF target Syria for the proposed preemptive offensive? Until 1967, Israel Defense Force plans targeted Egypt first. Ringed by four hostile nations, the Israeli concept was for one offensive at a time. Until 1967, Egypt had the most potent armed forces among Israel's enemies, and furthermore the distance from the Egyptian-Israeli border to Tel Aviv was less than 50km. Post 1967, Egypt still had the strongest armed forces of Israel's enemies, but by then the more than 200km wide Sinai Peninsula desert dunes separated Tel Aviv from the Suez Canal front line. Syria's forces were admittedly less potent than Egypt's, but by 1973 the Syrians were much closer to Israel's rear than the Egyptians. By 1973, the concept had thus changed from Egypt first to Syria first, hence the ILAF's promotion of Operation *Model* against Syrian air defense positions and then Operation *Ram* against Syria's air bases with a preemptive offensive on October 6.

7   The switch from *Model* to *Ram* has been put down to poor weather over the Syrian front-line deployment of SAM batteries. In some cases during the war, the ILAF's use of poor weather to reject mostly Israel Defense Force requests for missions yields the impression of an excuse for not flying missions that they preferred to avoid. It may have been that Operation *Model* was the ILAF's immediate response to the information about an imminent war. In April 1973, the ILAF informed the Israel Defense Force that 24 hours' notice was required prior to *Model*, primarily for reconfiguration of jamming helicopters and deployment of support measures. It is possible that a subsequent more orderly staff discussion realized that more than a few hours were required to prepare for *Model* and recalled that Israel's Chief of Staff had urged the prioritizing of attacks on Syrian air forces over attacks on their air defenses, instigating the switch to *Ram* for the proposed preemptive offensive.

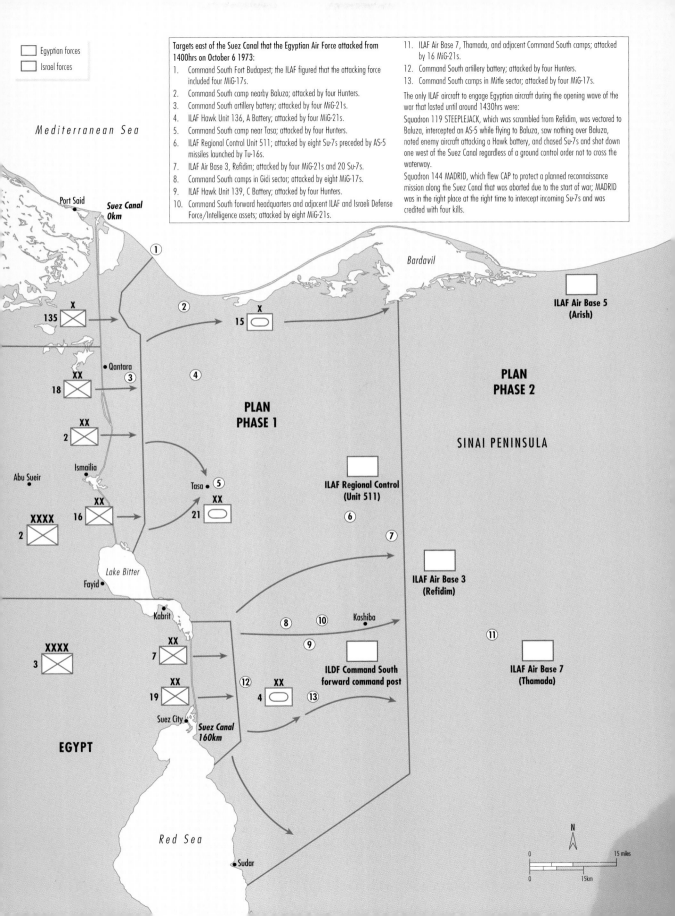

Egyptian forces
Israel forces

Targets east of the Suez Canal that the Egyptian Air Force attacked from 1400hrs on October 6 1973:

1. Command South Fort Budapest; the ILAF figured that the attacking force included four MiG-17s.
2. Command South camp nearby Baluza; attacked by four Hunters.
3. Command South artillery battery; attacked by four MiG-21s.
4. ILAF Hawk Unit 136, A Battery; attacked by four MiG-21s.
5. Command South camp near Tasa; attacked by four Hunters.
6. ILAF Regional Control Unit 511; attacked by eight Su-7s preceded by AS-5 missiles launched by Tu-16s.
7. ILAF Air Base 3, Refidim; attacked by four MiG-21s and 20 Su-7s.
8. Command South camps in Gidi sector; attacked by eight MiG-17s.
9. ILAF Hawk Unit 139, C Battery; attacked by four Hunters.
10. Command South forward headquarters and adjacent ILAF and Israeli Defense Force/Intelligence assets; attacked by eight MiG-21s.

11. ILAF Air Base 7, Thamada, and adjacent Command South camps; attacked by 16 MiG-21s.
12. Command South artillery battery; attacked by four Hunters.
13. Command South camps in Mitle sector; attacked by four MiG-17s.

The only ILAF aircraft to engage Egyptian aircraft during the opening wave of the war that lasted until around 1430hrs were:

Squadron 119 STEEPLEJACK, which was scrambled from Refidim, was vectored to Baluza, intercepted an AS-5 while flying to Baluza, saw nothing over Baluza, noted enemy aircraft attacking a Hawk battery, and chased Su-7s and shot down one west of the Suez Canal regardless of a ground control order not to cross the waterway.

Squadron 144 MADRID, which flew CAP to protect a planned reconnaissance mission along the Suez Canal that was aborted due to the start of war; MADRID was in the right place at the right time to intercept incoming Su-7s and was credited with four kills.

Mediterranean Sea

Port Said

Suez Canal 0km

Bardavil

ILAF Air Base 5 (Arish)

X 135

X 15

PLAN PHASE 2

SINAI PENINSULA

Qantara

XX 18

PLAN PHASE 1

XX 2

Abu Sueir

Ismailia

ILAF Regional Control (Unit 511)

Tasa

XX 21

XXXX 2

XX 16

ILAF Air Base 3 (Refidim)

Lake Bitter

Fayid

Kabrit

Kashiba

XXXX 3

XX 7

ILDF Command South forward command post

ILAF Air Base 7 (Thamada)

EGYPT

XX 19

XX 4

Suez City

Suez Canal 160km

Red Sea

Sudar

N

0   15 miles

0   15km

OPPOSITE SYRIAN PREWAR DEPLOYMENT AND ORBAT

The ILAF set in motion these operations against Syria because war was not expected to start out of the blue. *Scratch* was skipped. *Ram* mission orders were issued to the squadrons, while ILAF reserves were mobilized. Israeli squadrons received briefings for Operation *Ram* mission orders, with ILAF attack aircraft armed for offensive missions against Syrian air bases. Then, sometime after 1100hrs – only an hour or so prior to *Ram*'s H-Hour, with the first formations preparing for takeoff – the Israel Defense Force called off the ILAF's Operation

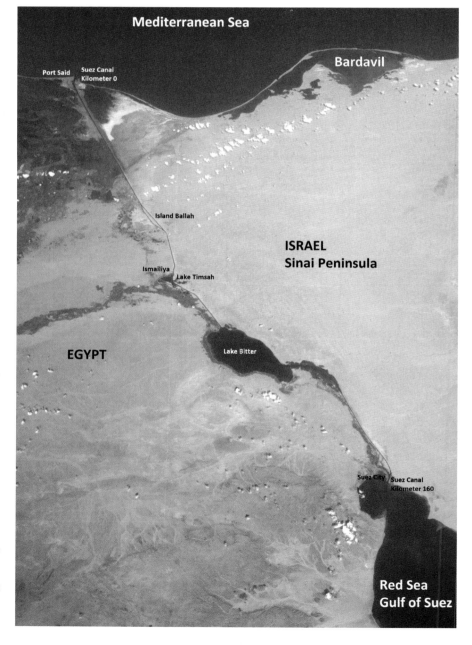

A closer view from space – also taken by NASA in October 1968 – of the Suez Canal front line that Israel defended on October 6, 1973 with three regular armored brigades. In routine readiness, these were deployed one at the front and two at the rear, but in high readiness they were to deploy two at the front and one at the rear to hold the line until the arrival within 72 hours of two reserve armored divisions. These divisions would counterattack to eliminate Egyptian accomplishments against the regular division that was outnumbered at least three-to-one in tanks and at twenty-to-one in artillery, with ILAF support to counterbalance the numerical inferiority of Command South's Division 252 against the Egyptian Second and Third armies. [NARA]

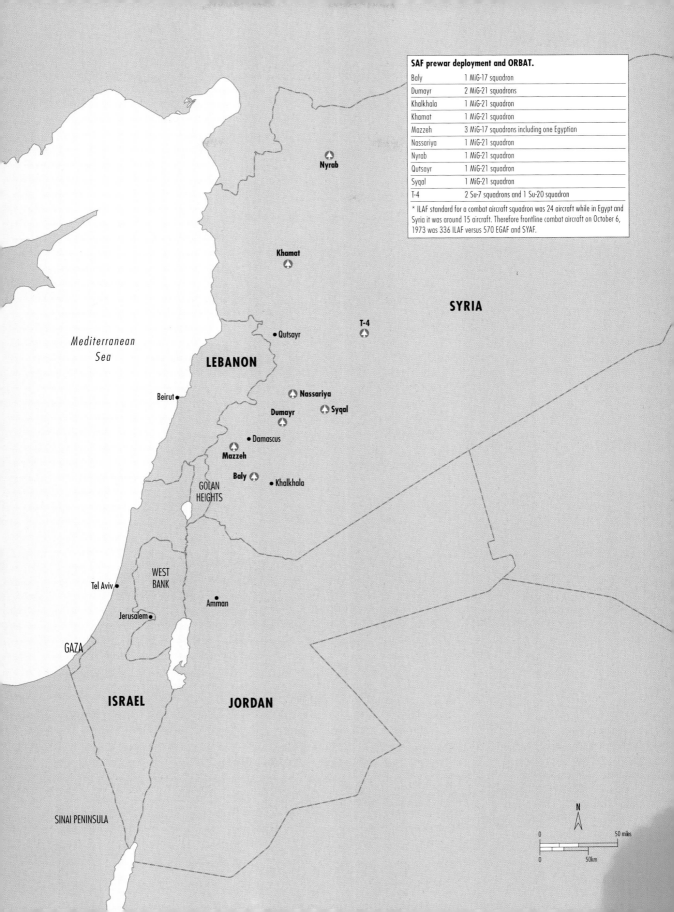

Nyrab ⊕

Khamat
⊕

SYRIA

T-4 ⊕
Qutsayr ●

Mediterranean
Sea

LEBANON

Beirut ●

Nassariya ⊕
Dumayr ⊕   Syqal ⊕

● Damascus
Mazzeh ⊕

GOLAN
HEIGHTS

Baly ⊕ ● Khalkhala

WEST
BANK

Tel Aviv ●

Amman ●
Jerusalem ●

GAZA

ISRAEL   JORDAN

SINAI PENINSULA

N

0 ————————— 50 miles

0 ————————— 50km

SAF prewar deployment and ORBAT.

Baly	1 MiG-17 squadron
Dumayr	2 MiG-21 squadrons
Khalkhala	1 MiG-21 squadron
Khamat	1 MiG-21 squadron
Mazzeh	3 MiG-17 squadrons including one Egyptian
Nassariya	1 MiG-21 squadron
Nyrab	1 MiG-21 squadron
Qutsayr	1 MiG-21 squadron
Syqal	1 MiG-21 squadron
T-4	2 Su-7 squadrons and 1 Su-20 squadron

* ILAF standard for a combat aircraft squadron was 24 aircraft while in Egypt and Syria it was around 15 aircraft. Therefore frontline combat aircraft on October 6, 1973 was 336 ILAF versus 570 EGAF and SYAF.

Ram against air bases inside Syria. As had been made perfectly clear to the Israel Defense Force during "Blue White," Israel's government was adhering to the policy that it would not start a war. Whatever the impact that Operation *Ram* would have had upon the start of the war, an ILAF preemptive offensive was no longer an option.

Still fixed that war would start at dusk and still prioritizing an offensive air superiority campaign over a *Scratch* scenario, the ILAF rescheduled an offensive against Syria's air defenses or air forces to the following morning and prepared for what could only be expected to be a relatively calm night for war in the air. Even if war was to be waged on the ground along the Suez Canal in the south and in the Golan Heights in the north, all three air forces – those of Egypt, Israel and Syria – were mostly geared for daytime warfare. The ILAF expected very limited offensive action from the aerial forces of Egypt and Syria during the nighttime, with just small-scale operations that Israeli interceptors were expected to counter and contain. Likewise, the ILAF was unable to generate massive close air support during the nighttime, especially prior to the accomplishment of air superiority when its attack aircraft were to fly loft and pop over SAM-defended zones, which was very hazardous during daytime and much riskier at nighttime. Then everything changed again. War started sooner.

Day 1, *Scratch*

Israel had been warned that hostilities would start on October 6. Egypt and Syria may have compromised strategic surprise by giving away the date for D-Day. It is possible that the date was considered impossible to conceal. Perhaps the revelation of D-Day was aimed at driving Israel to launch a preemptive strike that would have little impact upon the first day of the Egyptian and Syrian offensives, but would paint Israel as the aggressor, as the side that started the war.

What seems to have remained top secret was H-Hour. Egypt and Syria appear to have sacrificed the strategic surprise of D-Day to retain the tactical surprise of H-Hour. While Israel was expecting the war to start at dusk, Egypt and Syria attacked at 1400hrs. Although coming just a few hours earlier than anticipated, H-Hour's tactical surprise was overwhelming, practically securing the success of the first day of the Egyptian offensive and the semi-success of the Syrian offensive.

Egyptian and Syrian artillery opened fire at 1400hrs. Egyptian divisions then started crossing the Suez Canal in boats. Syrian armored forces began advancing onto the Golan Heights along penetration paths. Egyptian and Syrian aircraft crossed their respective borders to attack targets up to 100km to the rear of the fronts.[8]

---

8   The ILAF recorded that the Egyptian Air Force struck against the following Command South targets: artillery battery east of the Suez Canal in the north sector with four MiG-21s; artillery battery east of the Suez Canal in the south sector with four Hunters; camp at Baluza with four Hunters; camp at Gidi with eight MiG-17s; camp at Tasa with four Hunters; Fort Budapest with four MiG-17s; and forward headquarters at Mount Khashiba with eight MiG-21s. The following ILAF targets were also attacked: Air Base 3 at Refidim with four MiG-21s and 12 Su-7s; Air Base 7 at Thamada with 16 MiG-21s; Air Base 29 at Ophir with 12 MiG-21s; Hawk battery near Abu Samara with four MiG-21s; Hawk battery near Gidi with four Hunters; Hawk battery near Mitleh (possibly dummy) with four MiG-17s; Hawk battery near Ophir with 12 MiG-17s; Hawk battery near Refidim (possibly dummy) with eight Su-7s; and Regional Control Unit 511 near Refidim with eight Su-7s plus four AS-5 missiles. The Solomon Region Communication Center was also targeted by four MiG-21s. This meant a total of 124 attacking aircraft, but the number may have been higher as Egyptian Defense Force chief Shazly claimed 200.

0009065977

Sell your books at
World of Books!
Go to sell.worldofbooks.com
and get an instant price quote.
We even pay the shipping - see
what your old books are worth
today!

The start of hostilities at 1400hrs took the Israelis completely by surprise. Their Command South armored brigades were not deployed as planned for the start of war, while the absence of the chief of Command North may also have had an impact as the Syrians broke through in the Brigade 188 sector. The ILAF had been preparing for war since dawn so the expected start of fighting was not a strategic surprise, but the actual start time at an earlier H-Hour was certainly a tactical surprise.

Still, *Scratch* was not activated at 1400hrs. ILAF attack aircraft did not perform loft and pop operations over the front lines. Not a single Egyptian boat was attacked from the air while crossing the Suez Canal from 1400hrs. Not a single Syrian tank came under aerial attack while advancing towards the Golan Heights at the same time.

The ILAF scrambled interceptors, but space and time played against the Kurnass crews and Mirage pilots. Only four ILAF formations intercepted Egyptian and Syrian aircraft immediately after H-Hour.[9]

The opening offensives by the Egyptian and Syrian air forces were therefore successful, with damage caused to Israeli forces for relatively light losses among attacking aircraft. The opening air offensive also diverted the ILAF from immediately starting to attack the more important targets on the ground, instead chasing less important targets in the air.

An Israel Defense Force officer reported the situation to the Prime Minister at 1430hrs: "The intelligence information that we had referred to 1800hrs as H-Hour. This information was either incorrect or they [Egypt and Syria] realized that strategic surprise was lost therefore

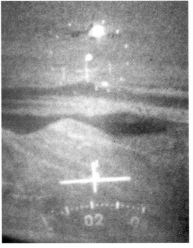

Squadron 144 MADRID 1's Nesher sight image during interception of an Egyptian Su-7 at around 1400hrs on October 6. The external stores under the Su-7's wings indicate interception during ingress, but all other Egyptian opening wave aerial formations penetrated unhindered because MADRID was the only ILAF CAP over Sinai at the start of the war. (AC)

9   Squadron 107 BED was scrambled from Air Base 29, the ILAF crediting it with seven kills: six MiG-17s and a MiG-21; Squadron 117 LARK was scrambled from Wing 1 and the ILAF credited LARK 1 with a MiG-21 kill; Squadron 119 STEEPLEJACK was scrambled from Air Base 3, STEEPLEJACK 1 being credited with two kills: an AS-5 and Su-7; Squadron 144 MADRID was flying a patrol mission over Sinai when war broke out, the ILAF crediting it with four Su-7 kills. Additionally, the ILAF credited AAA with five kills and Hawk missiles with three kills, while sometime later Squadron 101 FARID was scrambled from Wing 4 and intercepted and shot down an AS-5 that was probably aimed at an Israeli rear radar station, possibly Unit 501 or Unit 509.

Postwar, Squadron 107 Kurnass navigator Yossi Yaari visited the site – west of Air Base 3 Refidim – where the Mi-8 helicopter crashed that the crew of Goren and Yaari had shot down at dusk on October 6, 1973. (AC)

starting the war four hours sooner. I believe that this plays into our hands. We can exploit our air power during daylight..."[10]

The first ILAF offensive missions arrived over the front lines around 1500hrs, more than an hour after the Egyptian and Syrian H-Hour. These were not *Scratch* missions tasked to loft or pop against crossing points along the Suez Canal or penetration paths in the Golan Heights, but were more like what the Israelis called routine security support missions. In such missions, ILAF aircraft were assigned a target in the air while flying over the Israeli side of the border at medium altitude, then pinpointed the target visually, crossed the border, and launched an attack. Before dusk, the Israelis lost two Ahits over the Golan Heights and three more along the Suez Canal. The overall impact of these ILAF support missions was negligible.

Around dusk, the Syrian Air Force attacked Command North positions again, and Egyptian Mi-8 helicopters inserted commandos into Sinai with a probable prime objective of blocking roads to the rear of the front line in order to disrupt traffic of Israeli logistic echelons and to delay the expected arrival at the front of Israeli reserves. The Israelis identified four principal insertions encompassing an estimated 40-plus helicopters, from north to south:

- Mound Pelusium some 22km east of Suez Canal Kilometer 25.[11] The ILAF reported six Mi-8 helicopters flying the insertion. Saar formation GVATH,[12] which was flying a support mission when retasked to intercept the helicopters, jettisoned offensive ordnance and fired at the helicopters but missed. A Kurnass formation was also vectored to the north sector but the Kurnass leader intercepted the Saars and launched a Deker. GVATH 1 was hit, disengaged, and made an emergency landing at Air Base 5 Arish. Interception of the helicopters was then practically called off. The insertion at Mound Pelusium was thus accomplished in line with Egyptian planning. The Egyptian commandos blocked Route Hem to Command South's Fort Budapest until October 10 and ambushed Route Broomrape along which the Israeli reserve Division 162 was advancing to the front line, causing casualties and delaying the division's deployment.
- Landing zones west of Air Base 3 and ILAF Regional Control Unit 511 some 65km east of the Suez Canal Kilometer 93, with a probable objective to block Route Inn. The Israelis reported 12 Mi-8 helicopters flying the insertion in the center sector and at least six ILAF formations were vectored to intercept them. Three ILAF formations intercepted successfully, five Kurnass crews being credited with eight kills. It is unclear whether the helicopters were intercepted during ingress or egress, possibly both. It seems that at least some of the force landed scattered rather than concentrated at the planned landing zone(s). The presumed objective to block Route Inn was not accomplished.[13]

10   ILGOV State Archive 00071706.82.2C.28.0E.

11   The Suez Canal Kilometer count was from north to south, the canal's connection to the Mediterranean Sea being Kilometer 0 and the connection to the Red Sea Kilometer 160.

12   Squadron 105's Saar roster include more than 50 pilots, hence it was the only ILAF combat aircraft squadron during the October 1973 War with two general call signs: KIBBUTZ and SPORT. The specific formation call sign GVATH was in the KIBBUTZ group and was assigned to pilot Amiram Shaked, Squadron 105 Deputy B at the time.

13   Postwar, the Israel Defense Force pinpointed eight Mi-8 crash sites in the Command South center sector: two crash sites some 60km east of the Suez Canal Kilometer 93, a cluster of five crash sites some 15km east of the Suez Canal Kilometer 98, and one crash site about 30km east of the Suez Canal Kilometer 120.

- Ras Sudar sector some 40km south of the Suez Canal Kilometer 160 was the insertion objective for 18 Mi-8 helicopters. Kurnass crews were credited with six kills and Nesher pilots with two kills, while the Ras Sudar-based Unit 139 Battery A launched one Hawk missile and was credited with a kill. The inserted Egyptian commandos blocked Route Panic, practically isolating Ras Sudar from Command South to the north.[14]

- Abu Rhodes was an area of oilfields roughly 180km south of the Suez Canal Kilometer 160. The Israel Defense Force figured that 13 or 14 Mi-8s flew commandos to three landing zones in the Abu Rhodes sector.

After sunset, the Israelis flew dozens of loft sorties against crossing points along the Suez Canal. By then, five Egyptian divisions had crossed the canal, mostly unhindered by the ILAF. Two main bridges per crossing division were planned. The first Egyptian bridge across the Suez Canal was opened at 2030hrs. The impact of ILAF nighttime loft missions was minimal and one Kurnass was lost.

Egyptian Mi-8 helicopters attacked with rockets in the Abu Rhodes sector and Tu-16 bombers launched AS-5 missiles that homed onto the radars of Regional Control Unit 528 to the north of the Air Base 29 at the southern tip of Sinai. The ILAF claimed that Israel Defense Force ground fire shot down three Mi-8 helicopters in the Abu Rhodes area. The Tu-16s' action against Unit 528 was successful and the southernmost ILAF Regional Control Unit had to be replaced by a temporary control unit stationed at Air Base 29.

The Syrian Air Force attempted to attack in the ILAF Command North's Brigade 7 sector with a combination of an illuminator aircraft dropping flares for attacking aircraft, an attack profile that proved to be an anachronism by 1973, at least over front lines with proper ground-to-air defenses. Unit 138 Battery A engaged the Syrian aircraft twice, launching one

14   Postwar, the Israelis pinpointed seven Mi-8 crash sites in the Ras Sudar sector, though it is possible that Mi-8s also crashed into the Red Sea's Gulf of Suez to the west of Ras Sudar. The Mi-8 credited to the Unit 139 Battery A Hawk missile on October 6 was engaged during the egress of the helicopters at a range of some 12km west of Ras Sudar while the helicopters were flying over the Gulf of Suez.

ILAF Kurnass shooting down a very low-flying Egyptian Mi-8 helicopter

At dusk on October 6, ILAF Squadron 107's CLOSET and Squadron 113's OSCAR intercepted the Egyptian insertion of commandos in the Ras Sudar sector some 40km south of Suez Canal Kilometer 160. The Israelis' postwar report claimed that the Ras Sudar action had involved 18 Mi-8 helicopters tasked to insert commandos into two landing zones east of Ras Sudar. Postwar, the ILAF credited CLOSET 1 with five kills, CLOSET 2 with one kill, OSCAR 1 with two kills, and the Ras Sudar-based Hawk Unit 139's Battery A with one kill.

Shooting down helicopters flying low and slow was not as easy as might have been expected, pilots engaged helicopters either as air-to-air targets flying slowly or as air-to-ground targets moving fast. All eight credited air-to-air kills in the Ras Sudar interceptions were attributed to gunfire, but CLOSET 1 – Squadron 107 Deputy A Shlomo Egozi with navigator Roy Manoff in Kurnass 151 – added to one of the kills; after hitting the helicopter with gunfire, they made a pass over the doomed helicopter with a pull-up right above the Mi-8, coupled with activation of the afterburner so that the engine's thrust would push the helicopter down into the ground.

Many of the Egyptian Mi-8 helicopters shot down over the Ras Sudar sector at around dusk on October 6 were engaged during egress, because Egyptian commandos were definitely inserted and blocked Route Panic, practically isolating Ras Sudar from Command South to the north.

Postwar, the Israelis pinpointed seven Mi-8 crash sites in the Ras Sudar sector, though it is probable that additional Mi-8s also crashed into the Red Sea Gulf of Suez to the west of Ras Sudar. The Mi-8 credited to Unit 139's Battery A Hawk on October 6 was engaged during the egress of the helicopters at a range of some 12km west of Ras Sudar while the helicopters were flying over the Red Sea Gulf of Suez, so it almost certainly crashed into the Red Sea.

The ILAF's combat aircraft order of battle had enough margins to fly some *Scratch* scenario support missions in parallel with a major offensive operation. While most ILAF attack aircraft were committed to Operation *Challenge 4* on the morning of October 7, Squadron 105 SKI was tasked to support Command North in what was in essence a *Scratch* mission that was flown regardless of an opposing active integrated air defense system. At around 0700hrs, SKI 2 was wrecked in a takeoff accident at Wing 4, Khatsor, the pilot being seriously injured. SKI 1 orbited over Khatsor until a replacement SKI 2 departed, but this aircraft was lost over the southern sector of the Golan Heights, the ILAF attributing the loss to a Syrian SA-6 SAM. (AC)

Hawk missile at 2030hrs and three further Hawk missiles at 2220hrs, when two hits were claimed. The ILAF did not credit Unit 138 Battery A with kills, but the launch of the Hawk missiles may have thwarted Syria's aerial attack attempts.

From dusk until midnight, combat aircraft activity slowed significantly. Before dusk, Egyptian, Israeli, and Syrian combat aircraft flew up to 1,000 sorties within four hours. After darkness fell they mounted less than 100 sorties over the following six hours. Nighttime air operations were negligible in scale and effectiveness, the October 1973 War in the air being primarily fought during daylight hours.

Down south, the first day of hostilities had ended with Egyptian success. Five Egyptian divisions secured bridgeheads along a narrow strip of land – up to 10km wide – east of the Suez Canal. Bridges across the waterway enabled the movement forward of Egyptian armor and the crucial flow of logistics. The sheer size of the Egyptian crossing force within the supporting shield provided by Egyptian Air Defense SAMs was intended to enable them to contain the expected Israeli counteroffensive.

Up north, the first day brought mixed results for the Syrians, who had captured the Mount Hermon fort and penetrated the southern sector of the Golan Heights, but failed to penetrate the northern sector.

For the ILAF, Day 1 of the war ended with seemingly reasonable results, having shot down 21 Egyptian and Syrian combat aircraft for the loss of six of their own aircraft, as well as the generation of some 400 combat aircraft sorties.[15]

However, the ILAF's impact during the first day was far less impressive than the seemingly favorable accounting presented postwar. *Scratch* was not activated. The initial Egyptian and Syrian air force offensives from 1400hrs until 1430hrs shifted Israel's focus from attacking crossing points and penetration paths to chasing aircraft in the air. There was no ILAF main effort during Day 1, when its impact upon the actual conduct of the war was minimal.

15   Kills, losses, and sorties – unless otherwise indicated – are all from ILAF postwar analysis and research that yielded official numbers. Only the numbers of ILAF losses are absolutely accurate. The numbers for kills are drawn from ILAF credited kills (backed by an ILAF certificate), which may well have been higher than actual Egyptian and Syrian losses. The numbers for sorties are the official ILAF count, but their reporting standard at the time was not good and these should be treated as approximate figures. The numbers of attack sorties are more deceptive as the totals usually included missions that departed but did not attack, those in which not all aircraft attacked, and those that missed, so the totals reveal nothing about the actual impact of ILAF attacks.

Day 2, *Challenge* and *Model*

Israel's start-of-war objective and preferences were the destruction of the enemy military power, Syria first, and only one offensive at a time. The ILAF's prewar plans were air superiority first, followed by destruction of enemy forces on the ground in coordination with Israeli offensives.

Consequently, the ILAF promoted Operation *Model* against Syrian air defense units and Operation *Ram* against the Syrian Air Force for preemptive action on October 6. This was what the ILAF had planned for the morning of October 7, if the war had started at dusk on October 6, as Israel had been led – or more likely misled – to believe.[16]

Then plans changed. The Command North chief sounded calm and in control. The head of Command South seems to have been shouting out for support.

The revised ILAF plan for the second day of the war was Operation *Challenge*, which aimed to accomplish air superiority over the Command South front line through the destruction of Egyptian SAM batteries west of the Suez Canal. Operation *Challenge*, planned for execution during daylight, included three waves:

- Wave 1 in the morning was suppression of AAA defending SAM sites and suppression of Egyptian air bases from where MiG-21s might have been scrambled to defend Egyptian Air Defense units during subsequent waves.[17]
- Wave 2 at noon aimed for the destruction of Egyptian SAM batteries west of the Suez Canal.
- Wave 3 was an end-of-day effort to destroy Egypt's SAM batteries that had escaped destruction during Wave 2, but more importantly an extensive mining of Egyptian SAM sites west of the Suez Canal as well as all likely approach routes in order to disrupt the expected overnight reconstruction of these SAM batteries.

Air superiority operations were most effective within the context of larger military action rather than as standalone actions. If Operation *Challenge* had succeeded, then by the following morning the ILAF would have had air superiority over the Suez Canal front line and been able to support a Command South counteroffensive on October 8. However, a Command South counteroffensive was not yet set in motion by the time the Israelis ordered Operation *Challenge*. H-Hour for Wave 1 was set at 0645hrs on October 7, but there was no H-Hour for a following Command South counteroffensive, which was the preferable prewar context for *Challenge*.[18]

Prior to H-Hour of Operation *Challenge*, it became clear to the Israelis that the compromising of the prewar "Syria first" concept may have been an error. Command South lost the Suez Canal line, but an immediate Egyptian advance deeper into Sinai and outside the Egyptian air defense shield seemed unlikely. Command North had not yet lost the Golan Heights, where battle was still raging. Syrian armor penetrated the southern

16 At around 1330hrs on October 6, the Israeli Defense Force chief presented to the head of Command North the original Israeli plan for war, assuming that hostilities would start at dusk: the ILAF's Operation *Ram* to destroy the Syrian Air Force on the morning of October 7, followed by Operation *Model 5* to destroy Syrian Air Defense forces later that day, ahead of a Command North counteroffensive from October 8. During the first full day of fighting, Command North – and Command South – regular forces were expected to hold the lines with limited ILAF *Scratch* support.

17 The conceptual necessity of Operation *Challenge 4* Wave 1 has been questioned ever since.

18 The ILAF emphasized during "Blue White" that the activation of Operation *Challenge* was preferable prior to a Command South offensive across the Suez Canal.

Aircraft from Squadrons 119 and 115 raided Mansura from 0725hrs on October 7, tasked to suppress the Egyptian MiG-21s base in support of Operation *Challenge 4* with four Kurnasses armed with 36 bombs and six Ahits carrying 24 bombs. MiG-21s defended Mansura and the Kurnass crews were credited with two air-to-air kills, but Mansura was not suppressed, the ILAF evaluating that it was not closed for operations in the wake of the attack so the objective of the raid was not accomplished. (AC)

sector of the Golan Heights, but Command North was still defending the northern sector. The Syrian objective was to recapture the Golan Heights, but Israeli reserves were already blocking the four or five routes from the heights to Israel across the pre-June 1967 War border. There was only a slim likelihood that the Syrian armor that had penetrated the southern sector of the Golan Heights would advance west across the pre-1967 border with exposed flanks, past the Israeli route blockades and prior to accomplishment of the first-phase Syrian objective to repossess the whole Golan Heights. So while Command South had lost the Suez Canal line, Command North was still fighting for a foothold in the Golan Heights.[19]

19   Israel Defense Minister Moshe Dayan was first to grasp the situation. Dayan was the Israel Defense Force chief during the 1956 War and a true strategist. During "Blue White", he foresaw the exact Egyptian plan for war as implemented in October 1973. At the start of the war, Dayan urged the Israeli Defense Force to order the ILAF to support it during defense regardless of the SAM threat – essentially *Scratch* – but his view was not accepted. Dayan was also the first Israeli top-level personality to visit the front, visiting Command North, realizing the situation, and reporting back to the Israel Defense Force.

By the time that Israel reinstated the prewar "Syria first" dictum, the ILAF's Operation *Challenge* was already in motion and Wave 1 was flown as planned. A seemingly bizarre action was the launch from Dalthon of a Squadron 200 Chuckar salvo aimed against the Syrian air defense. Squadron 200 deployed to Dalthon in northern Israel to mesh with ILAF operations against elements of the Syrian air defense. Squadron 200 Chuckars were employed as decoys so that the enemy air defense system under attack would lock radars and launch missiles against them, rather than against the approaching Israeli attack aircraft. ILAF hearsay is that Squadron 200 was forgotten, not notified of the switch from MODEL to CHALLENGE and launched the Chuckar salvo on time to support an operation that had been scrapped, supposedly masking ILAF aircraft-flying missions 500km to the south over a different front line, against a different air defense force. The reality was less dramatic: the ILAF ordered the launch of the Chuckars to support ILAF attack aircraft that were supporting Command North.

Operation *Challenge 4* Wave 1 was flown as planned but did not impact the conduct of war; AAA emplacements and MiG-21 bases hardly mattered. The Israelis lost two Ahits, claimed the destruction of seven MiG-21s, and prepared for Operation *Model 5* with H-Hour at 1130hrs.

The decision to stop *Challenge* after Wave 1 and to switch to *Model* has remained controversial ever since as it supposedly demonstrated a lack of tenacity. If *Challenge* had been fully implemented on October 7, then the Israelis were supposed to gain air superiority over the Suez Canal front line to support a Command South counteroffensive the following day. Moreover, *Challenge* did not involve the whole ILAF order of battle, as some Ahits and Saars continued to support Command North. These aircraft faced an intact Syrian Air defense that had not been attacked in what was essentially a *Scratch* scenario, but flew the missions regardless. Tzali Morr recalled:[20]

I did not fly during Day 1. My first mission was nighttime illumination in support of Command South. Early next morning our Wing Commander Zorik Lev stepped into the Squadron 110 morning brief to inform us that the situation in the north was alarming. The Syrians had broke through the lines of the regulars and until the reserves would arrive at the frontline it was up to the Wing 1 Skyhawks – Squadron 109 and Squadron 110 – to hold the line!

No wonder we went ahead with what looked like a suicide mission to attack with napalm Syrian armor at the south sector of the Golan Heights. Napalm was dropped from very low altitude, 50ft, 100ft above ground level, and our orders were to fly the mission at the lowest possible altitude, mostly below 100ft above ground level, and if a pop up was needed to pinpoint the target prior to attack then the restriction for the pop up was to climb up to 1,000ft above ground level because we were tasked to attack within the SAM Defended Zone, the Syrian SAM batteries were still intact and fully operational.

We received our specific target in the air and I planned to attack from west to east but there were two problems. The flight from Ramat David to the Golan Heights was uphill climb and our heavily loaded Skyhawks did not fly faster than 400knts. It was also early in the morning and we were flying east into the rising sun. I realized that attacking from west to

20   Morr graduated ILAF Flying School Class 54 in November 1967, attended a Squadron 113 Ouragan Operational Training Unit course during ILAF Year 1967/68 Term 3, was assigned to Squadron 109 Ahit H from 1968/69 Term 1, flew dozens of missions during the War of Attrition, served as a Squadron 69 Kurnass pilot, and was then assigned to Squadron 110 Ahit E with appointment as Squadron 110 Deputy B (Acting) from October 7 after Deputy B Levi BarZiv had been shot down by a SAM while leading Mission 110/23 to attack in pop a bridge around Suez Canal Kilometer 150.

east was an error. I turned back and flew south to the Yarmouk so that we would attack from southeast to northwest.

The run in was therefore over Syrian forces. It seemed as though every Syrian soldier down below was firing at us, there were firing flashes all over the ground and I could actually hear the rounds passing by the canopy of my aircraft as these created supersonic booms. Then we got hit. First Number 3 reported that he got hit and I ordered him to turn west, to fly another minute at low altitude then to climb. Next Number 2 also reported that he got hit and I ordered him to follow Number 3. I also sensed hits during the run in but the aircraft kept flying normally, there were no warning lights and I pressed ahead.

Short of the target I climbed to 800ft, 1,000ft above ground level to have a look around, saw a lot of armor, dived to the deck and bombed but there was a lot of additional armor ahead. I climbed a little to 200, 300ft, dived, strafed and turned away, west.

Then Number 3 reported oil warning light on and no oil pressure but he was still in control so I told him to climb to 10,000ft while heading back to base. Next Number 3 reported that he was switching off the engine. All you had to do to switch off an engine in the Skyhawk was to pull the throttle back. However an engine could run without oil for 10–15 minutes and that was all he needed to fly back to base. Before he finished reporting I – and I think Number 2 as well – yelled not to. He immediately pushed the throttle forward and the engine speeded up and functioned until he landed.

While at it I formatted with Number 2 and saw that the right outer napalm was burning and the right wing was leaking fuel! There were agricultural fields down below so I ordered him to switch off the detonators, to drop the burning napalm immediately then fly to the Mediterranean Sea and there to jettison all external stores.

Meanwhile in my aircraft the hydraulic warning system came on but in the Skyhawk that was not much of a problem. I dropped down the landing gear manually, Number 2 confirmed that my landing gear was down then landed ahead of me.

My lesson from that first mission was that even if the target was handed to us in the air, then I should transmit the target to the squadron and there, on the ground, the pilot in charge of operations should select the type of attack, should plan the run in and retransmit to me in the air. In fact I did just that in my next mission later that same morning and it worked fine. As for our three damaged aircraft they were all repaired and were all flying the following day.[21]

Two Ahits and a Saar were lost over the Golan Heights before ILAF support for Command North was called off later that morning. In anticipation of *Model* and until that operation's completion, the ILAF suspended the small-scale support of Command North, so instead of intensifying assistance to Command North as requested, the ILAF decision to implement *Model* essentially stopped all support.

The ILAF's Contingency Plan *Model 5* aimed to destroy Syrian Air Defense deployment east of the Golan Heights, which included 25 batteries: 15 SA-6s, seven SA-2s, and three SA-3s. The Syrian deployment east of the Golan Heights was divided into three sectors, from north to south:

- Two SA-2 batteries, two SA-3 batteries, and five SA-6 batteries plus a regional command and control post.
- One SA-2 battery, one SA-3 battery, and five SA-6 batteries plus a regional command and control post.
- Four SA-2 batteries and five SA-6 batteries plus a regional command and control post.

The Syrian SAM batteries were in theory all mobile and could be relocated between sites, but most sites had been pinpointed by the ILAF during prewar reconnaissance missions and observation from

21   Interview with the author, December 2022.

Mission 109/1 departed Ramat David at 0800hrs on October 7, tasked to support Command North. Fire from the ground, hit the lead Ahit during bombing, some of the bombs did not drop, and the damaged Ahit landed back at Ramat David at 0837hrs, having flown the short-range mission with two external fuel tanks. During the June 1967 War, Mystères and Vautours flew from Ramat David to support Command North without external fuel tanks in order to maximize offensive load. (AC)

the Mount Hermon fort. Some SAM batteries reportedly relocated on the morning of October 7 to escape Command North artillery that bombarded SAM batteries whenever and wherever ILAF support aircraft operated over the Golan Heights, but overall the Syrian SAM deployment east of the Golan Heights was much more static and far less dynamic than presented postwar.

With *Model 5* being a contingency plan, it included options with guidelines for actual planning. The actual plan for the October 7 operation was a compact single wave that integrated suppression and destruction, as opposed to the separate suppression and destruction waves as planned for *Challenge*.

Support for *Model* included six Yasur helicopters and four Squadron 109 Ahits flying standoff jamming missions, Squadron 105 Saars spreading chaff, and Squadron 110 Ahits flying Egrof anti-radiation missions to engage emitting radars. Squadron 109 and 116 Ahits were tasked to suppress AAA in loft ahead of the main force attack.

The *Model 5* main force flew at low altitude in line astern, in what the Israelis called a train of formations. Each squadron's train flew to an initial point from where the formations fanned to the targets:

- Squadron 69 Kurnasses were tasked to outflank the Syrian air defense deployment from the north with 16 aircraft in six formations.
- Squadron 119 Kurnasses were tasked to fly a frontal attack across the northern sector of the Golan Heights with three crews to suppress AAA in loft ahead of 15 crews attacking a radar station, one SA-2 battery, and four SA-6 batteries in pop.
- Squadron 201 Kurnasses were tasked to fly a frontal attack across the southern sector of the Golan Heights with two crews to suppress AAA in loft ahead of 17 crews attacking two radar stations and four SA-6 batteries in pop.
- Squadron 115 Ahit Ns were tasked to outflank the Syrian air defense deployment from the south with a penetration route to the south of Squadron 201's sector and north of Squadron 107's route, flying in a train of five formations.
- Squadron 107 Kurnasses were also tasked to outflank the Syrian deployment from the south with five crews to suppress AAA in loft ahead of 12 crews attacking six targets, but the actual forces were four crews for loft and nine crews in four formations to attack four SA-2 batteries in pop.

The *Model 5* support elements and loft bombers tasked to suppress AAA functioned as planned and none was lost.

The Squadron 69 train of formations turned short of the initial point and the leading Kurnass flew into the ground, killing the crew. Nevertheless, at least one formation claimed destruction of a SAM battery.

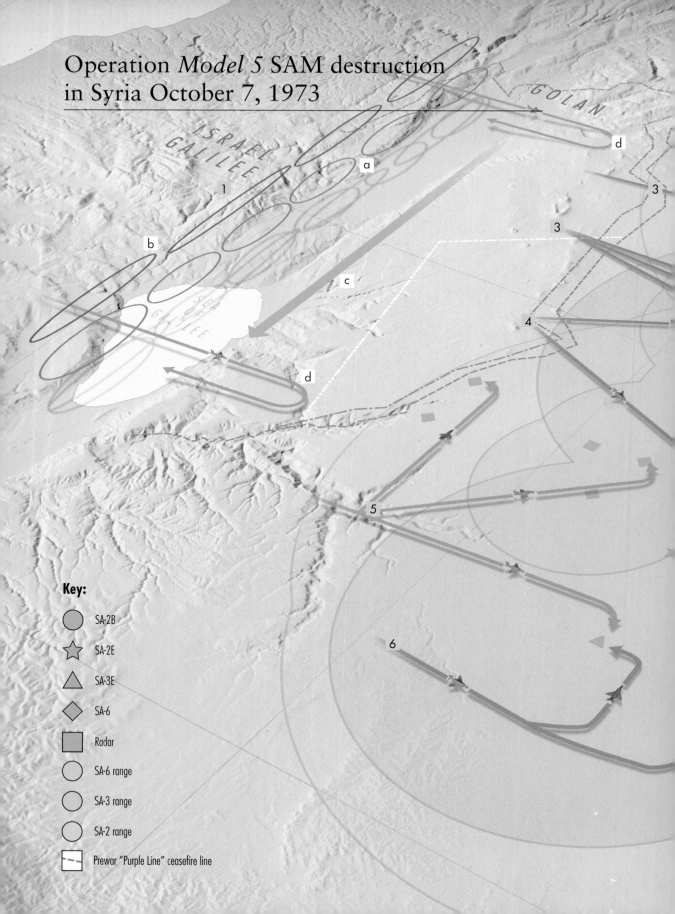

Operation *Model 5* SAM destruction in Syria October 7, 1973

GOLAN

ISRAEL
GALILEE

SEA OF GALILEE

a
b
c
d
1
3
3
4
5
6

Key:

- SA-2B
- SA-2E
- SA-3E
- SA-6
- Radar
- SA-6 range
- SA-3 range
- SA-2 range
- Prewar "Purple Line" ceasefire line

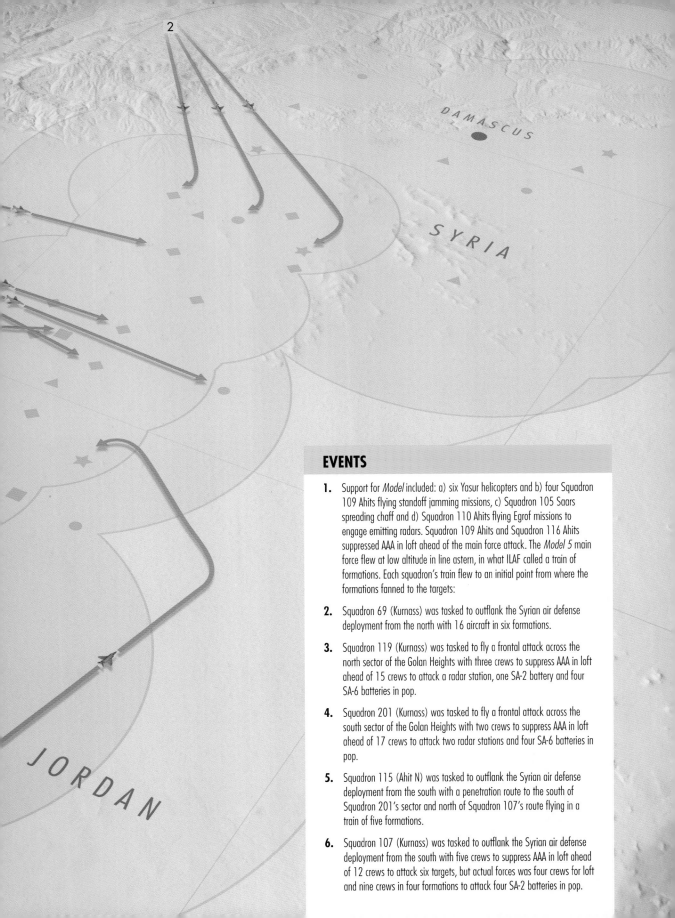

EVENTS

1. Support for *Model* included: a) six Yasur helicopters and b) four Squadron 109 Ahits flying standoff jamming missions, c) Squadron 105 Saars spreading chaff and d) Squadron 110 Ahits flying Egrof missions to engage emitting radars. Squadron 109 Ahits and Squadron 116 Ahits suppressed AAA in loft ahead of the main force attack. The *Model 5* main force flew at low altitude in line astern, in what ILAF called a train of formations. Each squadron's train flew to an initial point from where the formations fanned to the targets:

2. Squadron 69 (Kurnass) was tasked to outflank the Syrian air defense deployment from the north with 16 aircraft in six formations.

3. Squadron 119 (Kurnass) was tasked to fly a frontal attack across the north sector of the Golan Heights with three crews to suppress AAA in loft ahead of 15 crews to attack a radar station, one SA-2 battery and four SA-6 batteries in pop.

4. Squadron 201 (Kurnass) was tasked to fly a frontal attack across the south sector of the Golan Heights with two crews to suppress AAA in loft ahead of 17 crews to attack two radar stations and four SA-6 batteries in pop.

5. Squadron 115 (Ahit N) was tasked to outflank the Syrian air defense deployment from the south with a penetration route to the south of Squadron 201's sector and north of Squadron 107's route flying in a train of five formations.

6. Squadron 107 (Kurnass) was tasked to outflank the Syrian air defense deployment from the south with five crews to suppress AAA in loft ahead of 12 crews to attack six targets, but actual forces was four crews for loft and nine crews in four formations to attack four SA-2 batteries in pop.

Aircraft of Squadron 119 attacked mostly as planned and claimed to have destroyed three SAM batteries. EMPLOYEE reported seeing a radar, four missiles, and good hits, and subsequently claimed destruction of an SA-6 battery. JUDGE and POLICEMAN reported direct hits but POLICEMAN 2 was hit during egress, the crew ejecting over Syrian lines and being taken prisoner.

Four Kurnasses were lost by Squadron 201, the ILAF's narrative being that two were lost during ingress and two during egress, all to AAA. Israeli narratives blame Squadron 201's heavier losses on the route that its train of formations flew to the initial point, which was close to the prewar border. By the time of *Model*, most of Squadron 201's route over the southern sector of the Golan Heights had been occupied by Syrian forces. While it is true that Squadron 201's route was over Syrian armor with escorting AAA, it may well be that the main contributing factor to the two losses during ingress was the speed and not the route. Speed safeguarded Israeli attack aircraft during low-level flight over enemy forces, as it defeated SA-7 missiles and degraded the effectiveness of AAA. Kurnass pilots recalled that during *Model*, some of the aircraft carried up to 15 bombs and could attain the penetration speed only through activation of their afterburners. Syrian sources claim that all or some of the Squadron 201 Kurnasses lost during *Model* were shot down by Syrian MiG-21s, and Syrian aircraft were indeed present over the Golan Heights during *Model*. Less than 20 minutes prior to *Model*'s H-Hour, the Command North Air Liaison Officer indicated that Syrian Mi-8 helicopters were flying in the direction of the Golan Heights, with MiG-21s in the air to cover them. Six minutes later, the same officer reported Syrian air raids and Syrian helicopters approaching the northern sector of the Golan Heights. POLICEMAN 2 of Squadron 119 reported seeing Mi-8 helicopters during ingress, and Squadron 201's TIGER 2 reported evasive action against a very light-colored aircraft flying very low and trying to follow the Kurnass. The five Squadron 201 formations tasked to attack four SA-6 batteries reported mixed results. LIONCUB did not pinpoint a SAM battery during pop-up and instead bombed an AAA emplacement. DOG reported bombing the designated location but was unable to indicate whether or not there was a SAM battery at the site. DEER reported destruction of its assigned target. LAMB 2 malfunctioned, so in line with a *Model* guideline that attack aircraft should not fly alone, LAMB 1 followed MOUSE, but MOUSE 1 and MOUSE 2 were shot down during ingress.

The leading formation of Squadron 115 reported hitting an SA-6 battery, while the second formation reported destruction of an SA-3 battery. The fifth, trailing formation was tasked to attack an SA-6 battery, but reported an empty site which was nevertheless bombed.

The attack by Squadron 107 suffered from navigation issues somewhat similar to those of Squadron 69. CARPET 2 malfunctioned prior to takeoff, so CARPET 1 followed BUFFET. CLOSET's target was an SA-2 battery and reported direct hits. The targets of BED and ARMCHAIR were two SA-2 batteries, but BED did not pinpoint its target and ARMCHAIR reported an empty site. ARMCHAIR 2 bombed vehicles in trenches, but ARMCHAIR 1 turned back to attack an SA-3 battery that the crew noted during ingress and reported the destruction of the battery, possibly the same one that was the target of Squadron 115's DOUGH, an Ahit formation that also reported destruction of a SAM battery. BUFFET's target was an SA-2 battery, but BUFFET 1 spotted a SAM battery launching missiles and attacked that instead. CARPET 1, which followed BUFFET, also attacked that battery and recalled direct hits.

Operation *Model 5* has always been presented as the ILAF's greatest ever failure. The common story is that only one SAM battery was destroyed and another damaged at the cost of six Kurnasses, at a time when ILAF evaluation for losses in an air superiority operation against an integrated air defense system deployment was the loss of up to one aircraft per SAM battery destroyed. Field-level pilots and navigators have blamed ILAF staff planners for sending them into hell without up-to-date intelligence about the exact positions of the

SAM batteries, with routes exposed to AAA – especially in the case of Squadron 201 – and without proper support that was supposedly still committed to *Challenge* in the south. Staff-level planners, meanwhile, have cited problematic planning at some squadrons, navigation issues, and in some cases over-local initiative as contributing factors to the supposed failure of *Model*.

The impression at the time was somewhat different. During the first hour of Operation *Model*, available reports yielded an ILAF evaluation that 70 percent of the Syrian SAM batteries east of the Golan Heights had been destroyed at the cost of five aircraft lost or nine aircraft hit.[22]

At 1255hrs, the government's Israel Defense Force Liaison Officer reported to the Prime Minister that the ILAF had attacked 27 Syrian SAM batteries and that at the time of the report only nine out of 36 Syrian SAM batteries were active. An Israel Defense Force spokesperson stated that the ILAF had attacked the Syrian SAM batteries east of the Golan Heights and that most of the batteries were hit and were not now functioning. The Israeli government convened from 1450hrs, when the Israel Defense Force chief reported that 27 out of 36 Syrian SAM batteries were silent and that only a few missiles had been launched since *Model*. The chief then stated:

A Battle Damage Assessment camera image from a Squadron 201 Kurnass flying an Operation *Model 5* mission at around 1130hrs on October 7. The image captures Syrian forces on the move in the southern sector of the Golan Heights, including a T-62 tank, a bridge-layer tank, and – most importantly from the ILAF's perspective – a ZSU-23*4 AAA. (AC)

> We had a good photo of the Syrian [deployment of SAM batteries] and we went ahead [with Operation MODEL 5]. Nevertheless the locations of some [SAM] batteries were changed. They still have [SAM] batteries, I do not know where. The Syrians had 34 or 36 [SAM] batteries. Not all were destroyed. By tomorrow there would probably be 16-17 [Syrian SAM] batteries [east of the Golan Heights].[23]

Those who have labeled *Model 5* as a failure claim Israeli Defense Force and ILAF real-time reports were delusional and over-optimistic, with the supposed actual Model 5 results only a fraction – less than 10 percent in fact – of what had been claimed and analyzed in real time in the hours that followed *Model 5*.[24]

Whatever the case, Israel Defense Force priorities changed again even before H-Hour of Operation *Model 5*. Command South was again urging support against an Egyptian offensive deeper into Sinai, in what would turn out to be a false report. Down south, the distance from Israeli reserve bases to the front line was longer, so Command South reserves were not yet fully ready to fight. To the north, however, the distance from reserve bases to the front line was shorter, so by the time that Operation *Model 5* began, many Command North reserve units were already fighting the Syrians and changing the balance of power in the Golan Heights. The Syrians most likely did not plan to advance west across the pre-June 1967 War

22   Real-time reports were usually confused and incorrect due to the fog of war, but were corrected in later reports. The ILAF lost six Kurnasses during Operation *Model 5*. Two more Kurnasses and two Ahits were hit and damaged, but returned to land at ILAF airfields.

23   ILGOV State Archive.

24   ILAF History official research claims that one SA-3 battery was destroyed, one SA-2 battery was damaged, two SA-2 batteries were missed, three SA-3 batteries were missed, and 13 SA-6 batteries were not attacked. It is unclear what are the primary sources for the ILAF History official research summary of Operation *Model 5*, which contradicts available debriefs and reports.

border, at least not before repossession of the whole Golan Heights. During the second day of the war, the Syrian offensive effort focused on the northern sector of the Golan Heights with a frontal attack from east to west and an offensive from south to north. Command North repelled the Syrian pincer offensives regardless of meager air support.[25]

The Israel Defense Force probably expected that Operation *Model 5* would enable massive air support for Command North, but *Model 5* actually minimized ILAF support to Command North on October 7, and was not followed by an ILAF offensive against the Syrian forces fighting Command North; the Israelis actually flew fewer sorties to support Command North after *Model 5* than those flown before. Before *Model 5*, the ILAF History counted 59 sorties to support Command North at the cost of three aircraft lost; after the operation, it counted 38 sorties supporting Command North with one aircraft lost. Nor did a Command North counteroffensive with massive ILAF support follow *Model 5*; Command North was fighting the same defensive battle before and after *Model 5*.

Model 5 was neither a failure nor a success. It was an out-of-context air superiority operation, and as such was a waste of effort more than anything else.

Instead of exploiting the supposed success of Operation *Model 5* with massive air support for Command North, the ILAF's focus turned south again to support Command South with a prime objective to destroy the Egyptian bridges across the Suez Canal.

The Egyptians planned to have two heavy bridges fit for tanks per crossing division. However, it turned out that bridges fit for tanks were impossible to deploy in the southernmost sector of the Suez Canal, so eight bridges fit for tanks were deployed and the southernmost sector's tanks crossed over the two bridges to the north of their sector. Egyptian Defense Force chief Shazly stated that within 24 hours, the forces that crossed

---

25   From dawn until 0650hrs on the morning of October 7, the ILAF recorded only eight sorties tasked to support Command North. Until 1000hrs, the ILAF History counted 59 sorties. From 1000hrs until 1300hrs, the ILAF suspended support to Command North due to *Model 5*. From 1300hrs until dusk, the ILAF History counted 38 sorties for a total of 97 sorties that day to support Command North, including around 25 percent that did not actually attack. Full data from primary sources is not yet available but a representative study is Squadron 109's Ahit missions. Based at Ramat David less than 100km west of the Golan Heights, Squadron 109 started day two with a bizarre air defense dawn patrol, then flying six *Challenge* missions and two *Ram* missions. The first mission to support Command North departed at 0800hrs. Eight sorties in four missions were flown, with one mission attacking in the northern sector of the Golan Heights, two missions targeting Syrian tanks that were attacking from south to north along the pipeline route, and one mission attacking in the southern sector of the Golan Heights. AAA damaged two Ahits and only one formation reported seeing the launch of a single missile that missed, but that missile was most likely an SA-7, not a SAM. A mission that departed at 1040hrs with two Ahits did not attack, then Squadron 109 flew ten *Model 5* missions. From *Model 5* until the end of the day, Squadron 109 flew 12 sorties in six missions to support Command South and 20 sorties in ten missions to support Command North. Only three Squadron 109 formations supporting Command North from around 1300hrs until around 1700hrs reported launches of SAMs, one formation specifically stating an SA-7 and two formations not specifying type of SAMs, but these may have been SA-7s rather than SAMs. The Squadron 109 end of day report for October 7 stated 82 sorties with one Ahit lost during a Command South support mission and four Ahits damaged during Command North support missions.

the Suez Canal included five divisions with 100,000 soldiers, 1,020 tanks, and 13,500 vehicles. Occupying a strip of desert up to 10km wide along the east bank of the Suez Canal, Egypt hoped that the sheer size of the crossing force would secure its foothold in Sinai. Facing five divisions with some 1,000 tanks, Command South had one regular division with some 100 remaining tanks and two reserve divisions with 200 or so tanks per division. The regulars were worn out and in need of reorganization. The reserves were not yet fully ready to fight.

Command South was therefore at its most vulnerable point of the whole war. What particularly worried Command South were two Egyptian armored divisions that had not yet crossed the Suez Canal. The Egyptian plan was to hold back these two armored divisions until the outcome of the expected Israeli counteroffensive and ILAF attacks could be determined. If Israeli tanks were held up by the defense of the five divisions along the canal and if ILAF aircraft were decimated by Egyptian SAMs defending these divisions, then – and only then – Egypt would consider a renewed offensive deeper into Sinai and out of the air defense shield, to be spearheaded by the two armored divisions and supported by the Egyptian Air Force.

The Egyptian plan was known to the Israel Defense Force, but Command South had been shaken and the ILAF turned south to destroy the bridges that had already fulfilled their intended initial mission. The tanks of the five Egyptian divisions having finished crossing the Suez Canal. The tanks of the two armored divisions held in reserve to the west of the waterway were not yet supposed to cross.

The bridges were massive, modular, and repairable. Egypt's air defenses were still intact, and the defensive shield of the SAMs forced Israeli attack aircraft to fly loft and pop profiles,

Kurnass 115 from Squadron 201 – flying as 615 at the time – flew Operation *Model 5* mission 201/74 as DOG 2, tasked to attack a SAM battery site SD-4. When hit, the navigator ejected – with the ejection seat rod clearly protruding from the rear cockpit – to become a PoW in Syria, but the pilot – having evidently jettisoned all external stores – landed the damaged Kurnass at Ramat David, where the local Camel crane was quickly on site to remove the damaged aircraft so that the runway could become operational again as soon as possible. (AC)

OPPOSITE THE FRONT LINE AHEAD OF COMMAND SOUTH'S COUNTEROFFENSIVE, OCTOBER 8

The Israel Defense Force pinpointed Egyptian bridges across the Suez Canal on October 7, 1973. Also shown is Command South's bomb line as reported at 0215hrs on October 8, plus updates from 0350hrs and 0530hrs, with a third update requested at 0535hrs and approved at 0630hrs.

which resulted in less accurate bombings against the 13 bridges across the Suez Canal that Israel had pinpointed.[26]

Five ILAF aircraft were lost while tasked to attack the Egyptian bridges across the Suez Canal. By the end of the second day of the war, the ILAF claimed the destruction of 11 bridges.[27]

Again, the ILAF's action is difficult to define as a failure or success. In real time, it was seen as the only possible path for the Israel Defense Force to support Command South, with the ILAF generating optimistic reports. With hindsight, it was also a wasted effort. Too late to disrupt the crossing of the five infantry divisions. Too early to block the crossing of the two armored divisions.

26 Israeli Defense Force Intelligence reported at 1600hrs that eight bridges fit for tanks and five fit for lighter vehicles had been pinpointed, and that four of the bridges had been destroyed. The reference to destruction may be misleading and probably referred to bridges that were not deployed, possibly due to repairable damage. Shazly stated that Egypt had 12 bridges fit for tanks and that the plan was to deploy ten bridges, with two held in reserve, but the deployment of the two bridges in the southernmost sector ran into difficulties so eight bridges fit for tanks were initially deployed.

27 The ILAF report claiming destruction of 11 bridges was optimistic and misleading. Still, some damage had been inflicted. Shazly stated that the equivalent in parts of three bridges were lost, so the Egyptian bridging effort from day two onwards had to be scaled down from five deployed bridges and seven in reserve to five deployed bridges and four in reserve.

Egyptian forces crossing the Suez Canal from the west bank (left) to the east bank (right), with the Sweet Water Canal visible at the top left corner of this frame. At the time of the ILAF offensive to destroy the Egyptian bridges during the afternoon of October 7, the bulk of Egypt's Stage 1 fighting forces planned to cross had already done so, the main use of the bridges at that time probably being for passage of logistics. (AC)

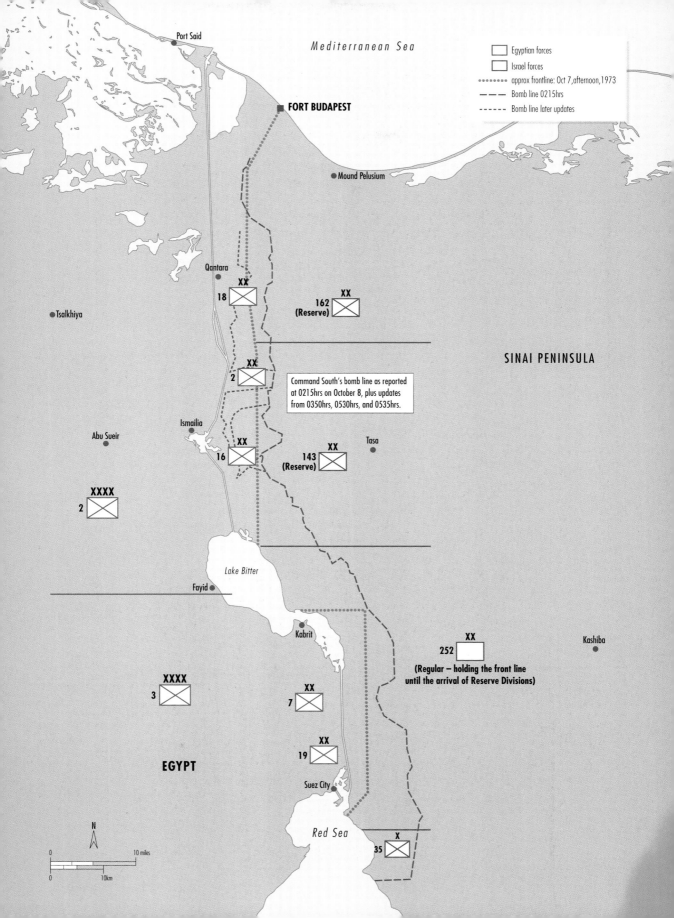

Port Said

Mediterranean Sea

	Egyptian forces
	Israel forces
··········	approx frontline: Oct 7, afternoon, 1973
– – –	Bomb line 0215hrs
- - -	Bomb line later updates

FORT BUDAPEST

Mound Pelusium

Qantara

Tsalkhiya

XX
18

XX
162
(Reserve)

SINAI PENINSULA

XX
2

Command South's bomb line as reported at 0215hrs on October 8, plus updates from 0350hrs, 0530hrs, and 0535hrs.

Abu Sueir

Ismailia

XX
16

XX
143
(Reserve)

Tasa

XXXX
2

Lake Bitter

Fayid

Kabrit

XX
252

Kashiba

(Regular – holding the front line until the arrival of Reserve Divisions)

XXXX
3

XX
7

EGYPT

XX
19

Suez City

N

0   10 miles

0   10km

Red Sea

X
35

Day 3, Israeli counteroffensives

Errors are inevitable during wartime. Contingency plans, if successful, may minimize mistakes at the start of a war. The ILAF ignored contingency plan *Scratch* during Day 1 of the conflict, and implemented three prewar contingency plans during Day 2: firstly *Challenge*, which was discontinued to enable *Model*, which was not exploited due to the switch to support Command South in what was in essence a *Scratch* scenario that came too late. The ILAF's impact upon the conduct of war during its first two days was thus minimal, regardless of it losing 28 combat aircraft.[28]

The air forces of Egypt and Syria flew few offensive missions during Day 2 and many more defensive patrols to protect Egypt's and Syria's rear areas from the ILAF, while Egyptian and Syrian air defense elements protected their respective forces along the front lines. By the end of Day 2, the Israeli Defense Minister reported to his government that Israeli aircraft had shot down some 40 of the enemy's since the start of war.[29]

By the end of Day 2, the ILAF had recorded some 1,160 combat aircraft sorties, and evaluated that the Egyptian and Syrian air forces had also flown a similar number of sorties during the same timeframe. The combat aircraft loss ratio was almost on a par, a lot less than the one-to-ten loss ratio in the air that the ILAF accomplished during the June 1967 War. The loss ratio was still slightly positive for the ILAF and was accomplished in the worst possible scenario for Israel, so there was still room for improvement along the timeline of the war.

In the north, the Syrian offensive had been contained. Command North had lost the Mount Hermon fort and the southern sector of the Golan Heights during Day 1, but the following day's Syrian pincer attack against the northern sector of the heights was repelled. The prewar "Syria first" dictum was reinstated in the wake of the Israeli Defense Minister's visit to Command North, and for Day 3 Israel planned a Command North counteroffensive. Command North's 36th Division's 1 Brigade would attack to the north of the Golan Heights to retake the Mount Hermon fort. Command Center's 146th Division would climb some

ILAF Squadron 69 Kurnasses raided Syria's Dumayr air base from 0720hrs on October 8, with the first formation attacking with cluster bombs, circular explosion patterns are captured in this Battle Damage Assessment camera image. One Kurnass from Squadron 69 was lost in the raid. The ILAF figured that Dumayr was suppressed for several hours, but the Operation *Ram* missions on October 8 did not destroy the Syrian Air Force and had no significant impact upon Syrian operations on that date. The ILAF monitored 293 Syrian air-to-air sorties and 81 air-to-ground sorties versus its counted average figures per fighting day of 291 and 38 sorties, respectively. (AC)

28   Fifteen Ahits, eight Kurnasses, four Saars, and one Shahak.

29   The postwar ILAF claim for Day 1 and 2 was that air forces of Egypt and Syria lost 48 combat aircraft, including 29 shot down in air combat, 12 shot down by AAA and Hawk, one destroyed on the ground, and six lost in accidents, including accidental shooting down of friendly aircraft.

1,000 meters from the Jordan Valley to the Golan Heights and would push the Syrians back from the southern sector of the heights.[30]

In the south, the Egyptian plan had been fully implemented by the end of Day 2. Egypt had five divisions deployed along a narrow strip of land east of the Suez Canal, where they were shielded from Israeli air strikes by air defense units. Two Egyptian armored divisions were held in reserve west of the Suez Canal to counter a Command South counteroffensive that would include the crossing of the Suez Canal from east to west in order to outflank the five divisions. Command South was indeed preferring an outflanking maneuver aimed at forcing the Egyptian divisions to retreat from Sinai over a frontal attack, and by the end of Day 2 was pushing for a Day 3 counteroffensive even though the two Command South reserve divisions were not fully ready, and regardless of Israel's prewar policy preferring one offensive at a time. The result was authorization for a halfhearted counteroffensive in the shape of a sweep from north to south along the east bank of the Suez Canal aimed at the destruction of Egyptian forces, a vague plan that Command South was aiming to evolve into a double spearhead crossing of the Suez Canal from east to west over captured Egyptian bridges because Israeli bridging units were not ready yet.

Egyptian and Syrian air defense units were still fully deployed along the front lines, so the Israelis did not plan ILAF bombings to precede the Command North and Command South offensives. Instead, the ILAF planned on-demand support. Two Squadron 110 Ahits departed Ramat David at 0532hrs on a mission tasked to support Command North. One of the Ahits was shot down and ILAF support to Command North was suspended.

In line with the "Syria first" dictum, the ILAF was tasked to precede the Command North counteroffensive with an air offensive against the Syrian Air Force to block any interference with the Command North counteroffensive as well as to destroy as many Syrian air assets as possible, which corresponded with the government's objective for the Israel Defense Force to win the war through destruction of the enemy's military power.

H-Hour for the ILAF offensive against the Syrian Air Force was set at 0720hrs. Some 80 Kurnass crews raided four Syrian air bases, encountering Syrian MiG-21s which at 0720hrs were flying defensive patrols. *Ram 11* coincided with a Syrian strike at 0720hrs in which Su-7s attacked Command North in the northern sector of the Golan Heights. The force committed to Operation *Ram 11* was too small to accomplish destruction according to the ILAF's own prewar doctrine. It was evaluated that the four Syrian air bases set for destruction hosted five squadrons or about 75 aircraft in some 75 shelters. To accomplish destruction by definition, the attackers had to destroy at least 50 percent of these aircraft. It was an impossible mission for the committed force in those days of statistical bombing under stress of war while fighting MiG-21s, evading SAMs, and engaging AAA. The four Syrian bases suffered hits to their runways, shelters, and infrastructure. Some suspended operations for hours pending completion of repairs. The ILAF lost one Kurnass in air combat and claimed that the Syrian Air Force had lost nine aircraft: six MiG-21s in the air and three aircraft on the ground. None of the air bases that had been attacked were destroyed.

---

30   The 146th Division was the only armored division assigned to Command Center facing Jordan. Since Jordan did not join the Egyptian and Syrian coalition as it did in 1967, the Israel Defense Force viewed the 146th Division as the only substantial high command armored reserve at the start of the war. Hoping that Jordan would not join the war and counting on the ILAF to destroy the Jordanian armor if it did, the result of the assignment of the 146th Division to Command North was that Israel had no more substantial reserves, with only ILAF to support the commands fighting Egypt and Syria.

Some ten minutes after the launch of Operation *Ram 11*, Command South requested that the ILAF stop bombing bridges in line with the plan to cross the Suez Canal over captured bridges. The Command South request was answered and ILAF support in the south practically ceased.

Israel's counteroffensives started almost simultaneously at around 0800hrs. Their general objectives seemed similar: to destroy enemy forces and regain lost ground. However, there were differences in the preparedness of the forces as well as the clarity of the objectives.

Command North had already deployed 24 artillery battalions. The 146th Division's push began at 0800hrs with massive artillery support: preparation fire prior to H-Hour, rolling fire during the advance of the armor, counterbattery fire to silence Syrian artillery, as well as utilization of long-range artillery to bombard Syrian SAM batteries and to fire chaff whenever ILAF aircraft flew support missions over Golan. The objective of the Command North counteroffensive was clear and simple: to push back the Syrians from the southern sector of the Golan Heights.

The 162nd Division started the Command South counteroffensive with the support of a single artillery battery in a sweep from north to south, too far east of the Suez Canal to encounter any Egyptian forces. The divisional sweep was to end with a turn to the west and a frontal attack towards the Suez Canal Kilometer 68 sector in order to cross the canal over captured bridges and then overwhelm the Egyptian Second Army from the rear. If the 162nd Division action succeeded, then the 143rd Division would follow with a sweep from the center sector to the south, followed by a turn to the west and the crossing of the Suez Canal over captured bridges in order to collapse the Egyptian Third Army from the rear. The objective of the Command South counteroffensive was vague and multifaceted. The Israeli High Command imposed upon Command South the practically pointless initial sweep. Command South added the canal crossing so that the attacking forces would have a real objective, but the two reserve divisions deployed were at the time mostly armored outfits without artillery, engineering, and infantry units, which had not yet arrived at the more distant Command South front line. There was no certainty that bridges would be captured, there was no assurance that the Egyptian bridges would hold the heavier Israeli tanks, and there were no Egyptian bridges in the southern sector of the Suez Canal; but even if the Command South action had resulted in a successful crossing, then the two battle-fatigued Israeli divisions would face the two fresh Egyptian armored divisions held in reserve west of the Suez Canal in anticipation of just such an Israeli course of action.

ILAF support for the counteroffensives was negligible prior to H-Hour, and was indecisive thereafter. Within an hour from the start of the counteroffensives, Egyptian Air Force units attacked key Command South assets, including Air Base 3 at Refidim, Air Base 7 at Thamada,

The ILAF plan for attacking the Egypt's Port Said SAM batteries on October 8 was to cross the Suez Canal at low altitude over Kilometer 20, turn north, and approach the batteries at medium altitude from the rear; it was believed that the Port Said SAM batteries were deployed to protect Egypt from Israeli aircraft expected to arrive from the north, from over the Mediterranean. SAM battery B-31 was not occupied at the time of the attack; Egypt had more SAM sites than SAM batteries, and batteries were occasionally moved between sites. (AC)

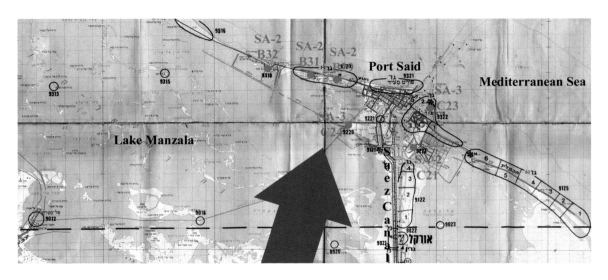

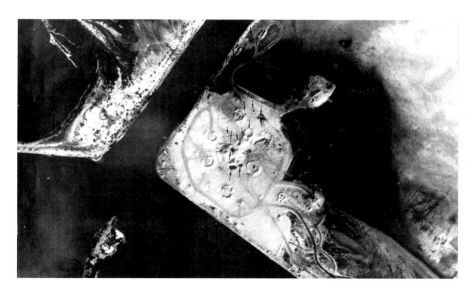

A SAM battery C-24 in an image taken on October 9 to assess damage caused the previous day during the ILAF offensive against Egypt's Port Said SAM deployment, with arrows pointing at bomb craters within the SA-3 battery's perimeter. There are many more bomb craters – unmarked – around and outside the SA-3 battery's perimeter. (AC)

Hawk batteries, and radar stations. The ILAF initially reported the shooting down of 16 aircraft, but most if not all claimed kills were engaged during egress, after the Command South positions had been attacked.[31]

Meanwhile, the ILAF focused on preparations to attack Egyptian SAM batteries in the Port Said sector at the northern mouth of the Suez Canal, with H-Hour at 1030hrs. Attacking these SAM batteries was primarily aimed at safeguarding ILAF aircraft flying missions deeper into Egypt, and for this reason Egyptian radar stations west of Port Said were also targeted at the same time. The Israeli Defense Force probably authorized the ILAF action in light of the bigger objective to win the war through destruction of enemy military power. Command South also had contingency plans to invade the Port Said sector, so anything that Israeli aircraft might destroy in the Port Said sector would have been added to the count of enemy losses as well as softening the Port Said area, which was considered beneficial for a potential Command South action if and when a relevant contingency plan could be activated. On top of the direct objective and indirect gains, the ILAF offensive against the Port Said SAM batteries seems to have been an operational evaluation to validate its prewar concepts and tactics for attacking integrated air defense systems through the targeting of a geographically isolated deployment of five batteries: three SA-2s and two SA-3s.

The ILAF attack on the Port Said SAM batteries went awry. Some attacking formations were recalled and ordered to jettison their bombs over the Mediterranean prior to returning to base, even though at almost exactly the same time Command South was requesting air support.

The ILAF decided to restage the attacking of the Port Said SAM batteries, with a new H-Hour at 1500hrs. Meanwhile, the Israeli counteroffensives were progressing in opposite directions towards an eventual antithetic outcome.

31 Postwar, the ILAF scaled down the claim to 14, comprising five air-to-air kills credited to Nesher pilots, three kills credited to AAA battalions, and six aircraft that crashed during that attack wave. The number of aircraft claimed as flying into the ground seems high for a single attack wave; there may be an overlap between the three categories of air-to-air kills, AAA kills, and claimed crashes, so actual Egyptian Air Force losses during the attack wave between 0800hrs and 0900hrs on October 8 were probably smaller than 16 or even 14.

The Command North counteroffensive yielded heavy fighting and slow progress, but was generally successful. Meanwhile, the ILAF reported to the Israeli Defense Force that the Syrian air bases had been devastated, generating an impression in the higher echelons that the Syrian Air Force had been suppressed or even destroyed, although Syrian aerial elements continued to operate over the front line.

The Command South counteroffensive initially generated high hopes among the high command, which somehow concluded that Division 162 had managed to cross the Suez Canal without a bridge of its own, with no substantial support from artillery, engineers, and infantry. In fact, the Command South counteroffensive was a shambles, which by noon at last became clear to the higher echelons. Division 162 had lost some 30 tanks in two separate battalion charges from east to west, with the tanks reaching or nearing the eastern bank of the Suez Canal only to be repelled due to lack of support. Division 143 started moving to its planned crossing of the Suez Canal in the southern sector when the initial reports from Division 162 were positive, but was recalled when the reports turned negative, only to find out that the Egyptians had occupied the key high ground it had vacated in haste. Again, as in Day 2, Command South feared a follow-up Egyptian offensive. As in Day 2, the Israeli Air Force was called on to target the Egyptian bridges across the Suez Canal.[32]

The ILAF pressed ahead with the replay of the operation against the Port Said SAM batteries. This time the attack was accomplished as planned, the Israelis claiming that two SA-2 batteries had been destroyed and three SAM batteries damaged. The ILAF concluded that the Port Said SAM batteries were out of action and followed up with bombings of various targets in the Port Said sector, none of which mattered much for the actual warfare in the south. With the Port Said SAM batteries out of action and ILAF aircraft bombing the Port Said sector, Egyptian MiG-21s were vectored to intercept them. The ILAF recalled the attack aircraft and vectored interceptors to engage the MiG-21s, losing one Nesher and claiming that four or five MiG-21s had been shot down.[33]

After the air combat over Port Said had ended, the ILAF returned to bomb the area while also attacking bridges along the Suez Canal. At around the same time, 130km to the south of Port Said, Egyptian MiG-17s attacked Command South positions, with Hunters and MiG-21s following in raids that lasted until sunset at 1718hrs.[34]

Massive fighting in the air and on the ground practically ceased past sunset, but ILAF tasking of Kurnass crews to loft against bridges across the Suez Canal continued.

32   Command South fears of an Egyptian offensive were derived from listening to Egyptian communication networks, so it could have been an Egyptian deception. The message was that the 2nd and 16th divisions would attack. Both were already fully east of the Suez Canal, so an ILAF offensive against the Suez Canal bridges was irrelevant, no matter if the information was true or false. Moreover, an advance east out of the air defense shield was in contradiction to the Egyptian prewar plan and would have exposed the Egyptian divisions to the ILAF in open desert ground. The initial Egyptian fixation to the prewar plan backs the assumption of a deception. Whatever the case, there was no large-scale Egyptian offensive at that time.

33   Postwar, the ILAF credited six kills: five to Nesher pilots and one to a Shahak pilot.

34   Postar, the ILAF claimed 12 kills over Command South from 1615hrs until 1715hrs: six MiG-17s, four Hunters, and two MiG-21s. The ILAF credited Kurnass crews with three MiG-17 kills and Shahak pilots with three Hunter kills, while attributing two MiG-17s, two MiG-21s, and one Hunter to AAA, plus one MiG-17 that flew into the ground. Again, there may be some overlap between the three types of claims.

Flying loft at night increased vulnerability and decreased accuracy. The *Scratch* scenario was essentially over, the Egyptian forces that planned to cross the Suez Canal were already in Sinai, and there was no Egyptian offensive action during the nighttime, yet the ILAF stuck to attacking at night and lost three Kurnasses in loft missions against bridges along the canal during the evening of Day 3.

Again, as in Day 1 and 2, the ILAF failed to make a mark during Day 3. The Syrian Air Force was not destroyed, the attacks on the Port Said SAM batteries had to be repeated, and interdiction against bridges in the south was costly and inefficient.

End of Day 3 figures seem to have indicated an improvement for the ILAF, which flew 666 combat aircraft sorties, of which 65 percent were offensive, versus 846 Egyptian and Syrian combat aircraft sorties, of which just 20 percent were offensive. The Israelis lost 11 combat aircraft and claimed that Egypt and Syria lost a combined 49 combat aircraft during Day

Israeli Defense Force chief David Elazar (right) visited Command North at noon on October 8, accompanied by Isaac Rabin (left), who was the chief during the June 1967 War when Elazar was Command North chief. (ILGP/PO)

3. However, the ILAF managed just 40 combat aircraft sorties tasked to support Command North, whose counteroffensive was the Israeli Defense Force's main effort on October 8, and this number was a gross figure that included aircraft that took off but did not attack, aircraft that missed their target, and those that attacked Command North units in error. Consequently, the actual effective ILAF combat aircraft sorties to support the main Israeli effort during Day 3 was probably half the number that were claimed, and possibly even less. If the ILAF objective was to destroy the air forces of Egypt and Syria, then claiming a combined loss of 49 combat aircraft per day was seemingly a progress of 5–10 percent in that direction, but even that ILAF count was somewhat vague and potentially optimistic, with room for some overlap between types of claims that included 24 air-to-air kills credited to Kurnass crews and Mirage pilots, nine shooting downs credited to AAA, three aircraft destroyed on the ground, and 13 that Egypt and Syria lost in crashes independent of enemy action.

The ILAF's cumulative claim from the start of war until the end of Day 3 was 120 kills versus 44 losses, but those claimed kills included more than 20 helicopters. Postwar, the ILAF claimed that the Egyptian and Syrian air forces had lost 99 combat aircraft by the end of Day 3, but on top of credited kills this claim included some 30 combat aircraft lost to other causes, ranging from flying into the ground to friendly fire incidents. The cumulative combat aircraft loss ratio by the end of Day 3 was therefore around two-to-one in the ILAF's favor, less than the Israelis had accomplished before and not enough for the destruction of Egypt's and Syria's air forces.

Day 4–6, Syria first

By the end of Day 3 of the war, the Israel Defense Force situation seemed to be stabilizing. Command North's 1 Brigade counteroffensive to recapture Mount Hermon had failed, but the 146th Division counteroffensive started to push back the Syrians. The Command South counteroffensive, meanwhile, had ended in both disappointment and disillusionment. The Egyptian grip along the east bank of the Suez Canal proved to be firm. Any Israeli action aimed at dislodging some 100,000 troops, 10,000 vehicles, and 1,000 tanks would have to be carefully planned and prepared, unlike Command South's hasty and improvised action on October 8.

CRAB and TIGER from Squadron 201 were tasked to bomb bridges across the Suez Canal at around Kilometer 68 at 1614hrs on October 8, around the same time that the Egyptian Air Force was attacking Command South. After the Kurnass crews released their bombs, they were vectored south to intercept Egyptian aircraft that were east of Suez Canal Kilometer 130, with CRAB 1's Battle Damage Assessment camera capturing TIGER 1 in pursuit of a MiG-17. (AC)

The Israel Defense Force therefore concluded that it had not enough power to win two wars simultaneously. The decision was "Syria first": Command North would continue to attack with the objective of destroying Syria's military power, and if it succeeded it might be possible to move a division from north to south to engage the Egyptians.

Meanwhile, Command South would hold the line and prepare for an offensive that would include the crossing of the Suez Canal in order to outflank the Egyptian divisions east of the waterway.

The ILAF's plan for Day 4 was approved prior to the Israel Defense Force's "Syria first" decision. The highlight was an operation aimed to destroy the Egyptian air bases at Mansura and Qutamiya. The plan also included an objective to destroy enemy forces on the ground, not in close support but in independent attack. The ILAF defined four sectors and assigned a squadron per sector. A formation would attack every 30 minutes regardless of the situation on the ground.[35]

A salvo of Syrian FROG unguided rockets hit Wing 1 at 0330hrs, sealing the "Syria first" plan. Added to ILAF missions for Day 4 was an operation to hit command, electricity, and fuel targets deeper inside Syria, with the aim of deterring Syria from launching FROGS and putting stress on the Syrian high command, signaling a change in Israeli policy and – hopefully – fortune.

From dawn, the ILAF initiated the new support scheme. Formations tasked to attack in the Port Said sector bombed from medium altitude due to an evaluation that the Egyptian Air Defense SAM batteries in the area had been destroyed. Ahit formations tasked to attack the other three sectors flew a combined profile, with a lead Ahit lofting cluster bombs to suppress AAA and two trailing Ahits flying pop to bomb the actual target. Within a couple of hours, it turned out that Egyptian Air Defense units were launching SAMs from Port Said. Formations tasked to attack Port Said thus switched to loft and pop. By 0715hrs the Israelis had lost five Ahits.

H-Hour for Operation *Ram* was 0715hrs. Four Kurnass squadrons were tasked to destroy Mansura and Qutamiya air bases. The ILAF evaluated that two MiG-21 squadrons were at Mansura and two squadrons – one MiG-21 and the other MiG-17 – were at Qutamiya. However, the assigned force was inadequate for the mission in line with prewar ILAF operations research, and *Ram* missions flown during days two and three had generated poorer results than expected. With hindsight, it can be seen that the mission was not accomplished,

35   The four sectors were Golan, Port Said, Suez Canal Kilometer 45–98 (Second Army) and Suez Canal Kilometer 120–160 (Third Army). The absence of ILAF Facs was possibly felt and might have prompted the change.

but at the time the ILAF evaluated that Mansura and Qutamiya had been devastated.[36]

Operation *Dominique* tasked 24 Kurnass crews to bomb three targets within a command compound in Damascus at 1145hrs, 1200hrs, and 1215hrs. Eight Kurnass crews were to attack two power stations, while four further Kurnass crews were to bomb a fuel facility. Two formations turned back due to low clouds and another turned back due to the confusion that the return of the other two formations had created. Only three formations eventually attacked, and one Kurnass was lost. Again, initial Israel Defense Force impressions were positive, but the actual impact has been difficult to define, as always in air attacks against targets that are not directly involved in the fighting.

Throughout Day 4, Egyptian forces pushed forward against Command South in order to improve local positions. Command North and the Syrian forces were engaged in a series of armored offensives and counteroffensives. ILAF pilots flying attack missions reported fewer SAM launches, and the Israel Defense Force speculated that Egyptian and especially Syrian air defense elements had consumed much of their prewar stocks of missiles.

SAM Battery B-29, an Egyptian Air Defense SA-2 battery in the Port Said sector, was photographed by the ILAF on October 9, seemingly destroyed after attack on October 8. However, the Port Said SAM batteries attacked on October 8 and claimed as destroyed were operating again the next day, demonstrating that integrated air defense systems were repairable. This also emphasized that offensives against integrated air defense systems were more effective – or even only effective – when in the context of a related military action – usually a ground offensive – rather than as a standalone action. (AC)

The ILAF end of Day 4 report to the Israel Defense Force was positive but bleak. Mansura air base was claimed to have been destroyed and Qutamiya to have been suppressed. The ILAF did not monitor a single Egyptian Air Force attack against Command South throughout Day 4, attributing this offensive inactivity to the impact of the raids against Mansura and Qutamiya, leading to promotion of a plan to raid two more Egyptian bases on Day 5. Yet despite fewer SAM launches, the Israelis lost 12 aircraft over the front lines but reported that only three bridges were still deployed across the Suez Canal as well as claiming the destruction from the air of 60 Syrian tanks.[37]

The bleak aspect of the ILAF report was the number of combat aircraft. It reported only 220 serviceable combat aircraft and urged the Israeli Defense Force to resume a Command South offensive.

However, Israel Defense Force thinking was to preserve the power of Command South and the ILAF until the two Egyptian armored divisions crossed the Suez Canal. The ILAF was therefore ordered to slow down operations in order to reduce losses. Support for Command South would be minimized and bombing bridges would be discontinued. Support for Command North would continue as needed. In line with the "Syria first" policy, the Israel Defense Force asked the ILAF why it should raid Egyptian air bases rather than those in Syria. The ILAF responded that the Syrian Air Force had already lost

36   The initial ILAF impression was that Mansura and Qutamiya had been destroyed. Infrastructure was probably hit hard but air base infrastructure is repairable. In order to accomplish its destruction mission, the Israelis had to destroy at least 15 aircraft at each air base.

37   The Israeli Defense Force was skeptical at the time regarding this ILAF claim, asking if their bombs could really destroy tanks. After the war, Israeli armor commanders claimed that a survey of 1,500 tanks that had been hit during the October 1973 War discovered that none had been destroyed from the air.

The ILAF raided Egypt's Abu Hammad and Quwaysna air bases on the morning of October 10, and postwar claimed that Quwaysna had been closed for five days. However, the Israelis also claimed the Iraqi Hunters flying from Quwaysna had attacked Command South on October 13. (AC)

100 aircraft, had only 180 serviceable combat aircraft, and thus was not posing a threat to Command North. The raid against the two Egyptian Air Force bases on the morning of Day 5 was consequently authorized and the ILAF was ordered to interdict the Iraqi expeditionary force.

Attacking a division-sized expeditionary force along a route stretching hundreds of kilometers from Iraq via Syria to the Golan Heights was an ideal mission for an air force. The ILAF tasked two Kurnass crews to pinpoint the position of the Iraqi expeditionary force. Unfortunately for the Israelis, the mission was flown just before midnight and missed the Iraqi vanguard that had already passed, as well as the main force that had not started to move. The Kurnass crews did not pinpoint any forces on the move from Iraq to Syria.[38]

Day five therefore echoed the previous day. Command North, with 250 remaining serviceable tanks from a maximum inventory of 600, was tasked to resume the push back from the Golan Heights of the Syrian forces that fielded some 400–450 tanks in the front line from their initial inventory of 1,200, according to Israeli estimates. Command South was tasked to hold the line and preserve its force, and especially to avoid the loss of tanks. Egyptian forces would continue with local attacks in order to improve their positions. Syrian forces would continue to engage Command North in armored battles.

The Egyptian air bases at Abu Hammad and Quwaysna were attacked from 0805hrs. The number of aircraft tasked to attack and the number of bombs carried were less than the ILAF's prewar plans for a raid aimed to destroy an air base: 20 Kurnassess with 100 bombs were tasked to attack Quwaysna, and 20 Kurnasses with 148 bombs to attack Abu Hammad. Kurnass crews reported hitting a Hunter on the ground at Quwaysna and two shelters at Abu Hammad, as well as damage to runways and infrastructure.

The Egyptian Third Army's 19th Division's 1 Brigade was tasked to capture Sudar, some 40km south of Suez Canal Kilometer 160. Israeli Defense Force Brigade 35 paratroopers defended Sudar airfield and its oilfields with a few tanks and ILAF support that became more efficient after the Egyptian 1 Brigade had advanced some 10km and exited their air defense shield.

Command North finally pushed the Syrians out of the Golan Heights, possibly prompting intensive Syrian Air Force activity. The ILAF counted 11 Syrian air attacks until 1000hrs, concluding that the attacking aircraft included Su-20s that were flying out of Damascus International Airport. The ILAF's Day 5 second wave offensive therefore targeted electricity and fuel in Syria plus Damascus International Airport and the Syrian navy's home port. Electricity and fuel infrastructure plus the port were attacked from 1140hrs, but the

---

38   Syrian MiG-21s intercepted the Kurnasses, and in the ensuing nighttime engagement a Kurnass crew claimed the shooting down of a MiG with an AIM-7 missile.

Damascus International Airport raid was delayed until 1410hrs and went awry, the target not being hit hard. In between these times, intelligence indicated that USSR airlifters were flying in supplies to Syria. The ILAF evaluated that the start of the Soviet airlift to Syria was in response to the scarcity of Syrian SAM launches and that the USSR was flying SAMs to Syria in order to replenish the country's air defense stocks. Israel's Deputy Prime Minister, Yigal Allon, suggested an attack on the Syrian air base at Nayrab, where the Soviet airlifters were expected to land from 1430hrs. The mission was authorized for after 1430hrs and four Kurnasses dropped 20 bombs at 1630hrs, aiming at the runways in order to minimize friction with the Soviets. The Kurnass crews observed four Antonov transport aircraft on the ground and one in the air, ignoring the airborne airlifter but reporting a taxiing An-12 as destroyed. Possibly in order to play down the significance of the Nayrab raid, the ILAF also attacked the Syrian air bases of Baly and Khalkhala at the same time, neither of which was hit hard.

Day five was a better day for the Israeli Air Force, primarily thanks to tighter Israel Defense Force guidance. Support was divided almost equally between north and south. Attacking the Third Army's 1 Brigade has been especially effective, and postwar Egyptian Defense Force chief Shazly wrote that the mauling from the air had destroyed it as a fighting unit for several days. Four Egyptian air bases were also seemingly out of action. Egypt's air defense deployment at Port Said was apparently suppressed and the number of Syrian SAM launches decreased considerably. The ILAF's claims-to-loss ratio slightly improved, with it losing more than 50 combat aircraft and claiming that the air forces of Egypt and Syria had lost more than 130, but the ratio was still significantly less than those the ILAF had claimed in previous confrontations and wars. There was also one major oversight during Day 5, as the ILAF inexplicably ignored the Iraqi expedition force that was on its way to the front line, advancing hundreds of kilometers along a route that was fully exposed to attack from the air.

For Day 6, the Israelis planned a Command North offensive into Syria, across the prewar border, in the direction of Damascus. The objectives were to destroy Syria's military power, threaten Damascus, and in doing so to deter Jordan from opening a third front line.[39]

Israeli air elements were tasked to soften Syrian forces prior to Command North's offensive H-Hour at 1100hrs. The seemingly successful strategy to massively attack two Egyptian air bases per day was abandoned. Instead, the ILAF targeted one Egyptian base and five Syrian

---

39   The Israel Defense Force deputy chief objected to an offensive into Syria, claiming that the best line for defense was the prewar line, that Command North forces were exhausted, that Syria would not be crushed, and that it would be better to prepare for the expected defensive battle in the south. The ILAF commander favored a Command North offensive, stating that the Syrian Air Defense was exhausted and reassuring concentrated ILAF support for an assault in the north.

A Squadron 113 Nesher reportedly photographed over the Golan Heights on October 10, obviously flying at low altitude, either while engaging enemy aircraft or after being vectored to intercept them, as it is flying without external fuel tanks; pilots jettisoned external fuel tanks only after being vectored to intercept enemy aircraft. (ILGD/A Bamakhaneh (in *Camp IDF Magazine*), photographer Miki Astel)

The ILAF attacked seven Syrian air bases on October 11, including Dumayr, where this Kurnass Battle Damage Assessment camera image was taken. The bombs of the photographing aircraft in the air at the bottom of the frame were probably aimed at the shelters captured at the top of the frame, when at least one bomb dropped by a preceding Kurnass had just exploded within the complex of shelters. (AC)

bases with up to eight Kurnasses per base, a force that according to ILAF prewar plans was barely sufficient for suppression.

Syrian SAM launches had decreased, but nevertheless ILAF support for Command North began with an attack against SAM batteries that covered the planned penetration route in the northern sector of the Golan Heights. SAM launches over the Golan Heights increased from the start of ILAF support at around 0800hrs. By 1100hrs, the Israelis had lost five Ahits, one Saar, and one air observation post Dornier 27.

Throughout the day, the ILAF continued to attack Syrian Air Defense batteries, raid Syrian air bases, and support Command North, but the Israeli Defense Force offensive failed to crush Syria. The distance from Command North's penetration point to the outskirts of Damascus was less than 50km. An Israeli invasion of Damascus was obviously a faked threat, but they hoped that an advance towards the Syrian capital, coupled with the destruction of Syria's military power, would force Syria to seek a ceasefire. None of that was accomplished by the end of Day 6. Command North's 36th Division advanced less than 10km from the penetration point against stiffening Syrian defense. Although Syria's military power was devastated, it was not destroyed; and a fresh expedition force was on its way to the front line, unhindered by the ILAF, along the long route from Iraq.

Day 7–8, ILAF low, IDF high

Israel was seemingly at a dead end. Command North had regained ground lost in the Golan Heights but not the Mount Hermon fort, and the offensive into Syria had started to generate front lines that would be problematic for postwar positions. Command South was waiting for the crossing of the two Egyptian armored divisions and any premature action was considered too risky. The Israeli Defense Force hoped that a Syrian plea for help would stimulate Egypt to attack Command South, but this did not seem to have happened. Then the ILAF instigated a shockwave of events that changed the course of the war.

The ILAF commander presented ILAF plans for October 12 from 0100hrs to the Israeli Defense Force chief. The ILAF plan was for two waves plus support for the ongoing Command North offensive. The first wave was a *Ram* mission against seven Syrian air bases and attacks on two Syrian SAM batteries. The second wave would target the Egyptian Air Defense deployment at Port Said that had supposedly been suppressed on October 8, but was launching SAMs again on October 11.

The Israel Defense Force authorized the ILAF plans, but what startled the Israel Defense Force was ILAF's claim that it would be down to 223 combat aircraft at dawn on Day 7. The ILAF's red line was viewed as 220 combat aircraft; it was accepted that with less than 220 combat aircraft, the ILAF would not be able to support Israeli forces' offensives. The ILAF commander concluded from the presented order of battle crisis that the Israelis should start an offensive in the south within 24 hours, before the number of combat aircraft dipped below 220.[40]

40   The ILAF's actual order of battle at 0600hrs on October 12 was 258 serviceable combat aircraft: 63 Kurnasses, 64 Mirages, 115 Ahits, and 16 Saars. Unserviceable combat aircraft at field level included 14 Kurnasses, one Mirage, and 18 Ahits. There was thus no ILAF order of battle crisis.

The Israeli Defense Force view until that time was that attacking in the south too soon was too risky. The alleged ILAF order of battle crisis changed the situation. The only Israeli reserve force from October 8 was the ILAF; without it as a proper offensive force, the Israel Defense Force would not be able to support a Command North or a Command South offensive, nor respond with ILAF support to a crisis in Command North or Command South. Without the ILAF as an effective reserve force and in light of the then balance of power in the north and the south, winning the war would be impossible.

The Israeli Defense Force chief therefore accepted the ILAF commander's conclusion that the best path forward was an offensive in the south. The issue was what would happen after that offensive. The Command North offensive had gained ground, but had not crushed Syria. If a Command South offensive also ended up gaining ground without crushing Egypt, then Israel would have had to continue fighting Egypt without the ILAF as a viable force since its order of battle would surely have dropped below the red line after supporting an attack by Command South. Israel's Chief of Staff concluded that a ceasefire would be Israel's best option; one from October 14 would enable the Israelis to launch one more offensive, by Command South, before the ILAF order of battle fell below 220 combat aircraft.

The Israel Defense Force chief's conclusion was discussed in a high command meeting from morning until noon. There seemed to be no better option. Israel would ask for ceasefire from October 14. If a ceasefire could be set for that date, then Command South would start an offensive to cross the Suez Canal with two divisions. The offensive would hopefully gain ground west of the Suez Canal to counterbalance the Egyptian foothold east of the waterway. The preset ceasefire would then end the Command South offensive before the two Egyptian armored divisions could counterattack and before the ILAF order of battle sank too deep below the 220 red line.

The Israeli government convened from 1430hrs to discuss the Israeli Defense Force chief's conclusion. Israel's Chief of Staff first outlined the situation in the north, where Command North was advancing but slowly and Syria's military forces were not expected to crumble. The ILAF had claimed the shooting down of 26 Syrian aircraft since Day 7 started, but the Syrian Air Force was still active and had been attacking Command North. The Israeli Defense Force chief then presented the implications of the ILAF's supposed order of battle crisis and the proposed path forward: a Command South offensive that would end in a ceasefire. The Israeli government tended to accept his conclusion, but then received intelligence information that changed the situation again: Egypt was planning an offensive that would start on October 13 or 14.[41]

The Israelis' preferred scenario has been set in motion. The two Egyptian armored divisions would cross the Suez Canal and Egypt would attack Command South with about 900 tanks. If Command South's 600 tanks could destroy hundreds of Egyptian tanks, then Command South would launch a counteroffensive to cross the Suez Canal. The defense against the

Syrian SA-2 battery photographed by an ILAF Kurnass on October 12, with a deployment of rear echelon vehicles protected by trenches against air attacks and artillery bombardments. The October 1973 War's battlefields and rear areas were littered with tens of thousands of targets, rendering the Israeli objective to win the war through destruction of enemy military hardware a challenge; obviously the core targets were tanks. (AC)

41   Around midday on October 12, Egyptian Defense Minister Ismail ordered Egyptian Defense Force chief Shazly to launch an offensive in Sinai on October 13. Within a few hours, the intelligence information that Egypt would launch this offensive was presented to the Israeli government!

Command North's pushback of Syrian forces from the Golan Heights produced scenes of abandoned tanks, but most if not all had been hit from the ground – not the air – during heavy fighting that yielded massive losses to both sides. (ILGP/PO)

expected Egyptian offensive and the possible Command South counteroffensive would still have to be Israel's final effort in the war due to the ILAF's numbers crisis. The Israeli Defense Force still requested a ceasefire that would set an ending to the war. The Israeli government accepted this view, and at 1730hrs Israel notified the USA accordingly.

The news that Israel was seeking a ceasefire surprised the USA, whose objective was a clear Israeli victory that might move Egypt from USSR towards the USA. Washington was well aware that fighting was tough, but until then Israel was promising imminent victory and asking the USA to stall ceasefire initiatives. To avoid losing face, Washington asked the UK to pretend to act as mediator and to ask Egypt for agreement to a ceasefire based on an assurance that Israel had already accepted such a proposal.

Meanwhile, the Iraqi expeditionary force had arrived at the Golan Heights front line and attacked the southern flank of the Command North penetration route into Syria. The Iraqi attack was repelled, but Israeli aerial forces had missed the opportunity to attack the Iraqi expeditionary force along the way to the front line and the balance of power in the north had now changed.

Intelligence indicated that the Egyptian offensive would launch with an insertion of commandos and paratroopers. The ILAF's proposal for Day 8 therefore included raids against Egyptian airlift planes and helicopters. However, the Israeli Defense Force rejected the proposal on the grounds that Israel was waiting for the Egyptian offensive so any premature ILAF action might have alerted Egypt to realize that Israel had advance warning of the attack. Egypt might then have canceled the offensive, which was not in the Israelis' interest. Consequently, the Israeli Defense Force authorized the ILAF's main effort for Day 8 as raiding Syrian air bases and supporting Command North, with a secondary effort to provide minimum support for Command South and to attack the Port Said sector.[42]

The ILAF began attacking the Syrian air base at Mazzeh earlier than usual in order to preempt MiG-17 action against Command North. However, raiding airfields just after sunrise at 0542hrs instead of after 0700hrs proved problematic. One formation did not attack due to a low glaring sun, while another attacked with only two Kurnasses, of which one was lost. The main attack followed from 0705hrs and targeted six Syrian air bases. Twenty Kurnass crews raided five bases, aiming at runways with an objective to accomplish suppression. One Kurnass was lost during ingress and 15 Kurnasses bombed four bases that

42   The ILAF commander reasoned that attacking Port Said would keep it clear of SAM batteries and enable the safe passage of Israeli aircraft flying missions against Egypt's rear, as well as accomplish the Israeli Defense Force's objective to soften Port Said ahead of a potential Command South offensive there. The Israeli Defense Force chief responded that the ILAF should not attack Port Said as a Defense Force objective, but authorized attacking the area as an ILAF objective during Day 8.

were suppressed for up to eight hours, according to ILAF monitoring. The Syrian air base at Mazzeh was raided by 12 Ahits.

At around 1300hrs, Egyptian Air Defense units and the ILAF tracked a target flying high and fast over Egypt, Israel, and Syria. Israel's agreement to a ceasefire had probably puzzled the USA, which tasked an SR-71 Blackbird spy plane to have a look at what was really going on. US image interpretation pinpointed 444 Israeli tanks facing 835 Egyptian tanks along the Suez Canal, and 419 Israeli tanks opposing 339 Syrian tanks in the Golan Heights.

Egypt's President Sadat then met the British Ambassador. The confidential information that Israel was seeking a ceasefire was felt to probably signal Israeli weakness and possibly forged President Sadat's will to go ahead with an offensive deeper into Sinai, against the opinion of Egyptian Defense Force chief Shazly. US evaluation has been that the USSR was pressing for a ceasefire to maximize Egyptian gains and minimize Syrian losses, so the Egyptian rejection of the ceasefire proposition stunned Washington.[43]

From a US perspective, the only path forward would be to impose a ceasefire upon Egypt through an Israeli military victory. A USAF airlift to Israel would spur Israel to win the war and demonstrate to the world the USA's superiority over the USSR: US airlifters could fly farther than those of the Soviets, demonstrating their tank delivery capabilities, and would within a short while outpace the USSR airlift in delivery of total tonnage.

It was therefore the faked ILAF order of battle crisis that set in motion a series of events initially aimed at ending the war within the shortest possible timeframe, but which eventually prolonged the conflict to suit a US objective.[44]

Day 9–19, Israeli offensives

The final phase of the war was the longest: 11 days that started with an Egyptian offensive and continued with Israeli offensives until America's objective of a USSR plea for ceasefire was accomplished.

The SA-6 was a new system in October 1973, meaning many characteristics were unknown at the time. At the start of the war, the ILAF had no countermeasures so the Israelis prioritized capturing one, but being a fully mobile system – unlike the semi-mobile SA-3 and mostly static SA-2 – Egyptian and Syrian SA-6 batteries evaded capture and the ILAF had to settle for parts collected on battlefields, including this rear part of a missile that was reportedly photographed on October 13. The image illustrates the harsh terrain of the Golan Heights, which was a challenge to armored mobility and mostly forced it along passable roads and tracks, spreading along ridges only when the terrain enabled wider deployment. (ILGP/PO)

43 Postwar, US Secretary of State Henry Kissinger claimed that the British asked the wrong question: the British should have asked "Would they accept a ceasefire, not would they seek it." The terminology used was also deceptive. Israel's intention was that the ceasefire's implementation time would be at the end of a Command South offensive to cross the Suez Canal in order to change the situation at the time of the agreement to a ceasefire.

44 In the words of the US Secretary of State: "On October 13 it was clear that the Soviets could not deliver the Egyptians to what was in effect a ceasefire in place, and to which we had obtained Israeli acquiescence, more or less. When that occurred we felt we had no choice except to go another route, namely to prove to the Soviets that we could match strategically anything they could put in the Middle East, and that we could put it into more capable hands. And that therefore the longer the war would go on, the more likely would be a situation in which they would have to ask for a ceasefire rather than we." (FRUS)

The appearance over the front line of Egyptian Mirages on the morning of October 14 – previously the Israelis did not encounter enemy Mirages – prompted the ILAF to paint black-outlined yellow identification triangles over its Neshers and Shahaks. (AC)

Day 9, Egyptian offensive

The ILAF's actual order of battle on the morning of October 14 included 281 combat aircraft at squadron, wing, and base levels, including 257 that were serviceable.[45]

The Israeli Defense Force anticipated nighttime commando raids and paratrooper assaults to precede the Egyptian armored offensive, so the mostly daytime Nesher readiness flight had been evacuated from Refidim. But there were no large-scale commando raids and paratrooper assaults ahead of the Egyptian offensive, which started at 0600hrs with 400 tanks and 13 aircraft attacking east against the rising sun. A Tu-16 launched two AS-5 missiles that homed onto the radiating Regional Control Unit 511 and disabled the radar station for hours. Eight Mirages from Tanta and four MiG-17s from Tsalkhiya followed. The ILAF therefore responded with retaliatory raids against Tsalkhiya and Tanta.

Day 9, *Ram 8*, Tsalkhiya

Tsalkhiya was a forward Egyptian Air Force base at the rear of the Second Army only some 30km west of the Suez Canal Kilometer 50. The ILAF counted 60 MiG-17 offensive sorties from Tsalkhiya and claimed that eight of them had been shot down by the morning of October 14.[46]

In line with prewar plans, the ILAF initially prioritized MiG-21 bases, so Tsalkhiya was not raided until October 11. Four Kurnasses were tasked to loft cluster bombs ahead of four Kurnasses tasked to pop. MiG-21s intercepted the loft Kurnasses that as a result did not attack Tsalkhiya but claimed two MiG-21s shot down. The pop Kurnasses attacked and the ILAF concluded that Tsalkhiya had been suppressed for 24 hours, not monitoring any takeoffs from Tsalkhiya until the morning of October 12.

The objective of the mission on October 14 seems to have been destruction, so the attacking force was larger, but not large enough for an air base destruction mission as defined in the ILAF's prewar plans. Four Kurnasses were tasked to loft cluster bombs ahead of four Kurnasses and eight Ahits tasked to pop runways and shelters with 32 and 40 bombs respectively. Eight bombs per Kurnass and five bombs per Ahit – regardless of the relatively short range to the target – were fewer than the ten bombs per aircraft as defined in the ILAF's prewar plans for an air base destruction mission.

Notwithstanding, the ILAF viewed the mission as extremely successful, possibly the most successful Israeli air base attack mission during the entire war. The Egyptian Air Force vectored 12 MiG-21s to intercept the incoming Israeli intruders. All ILAF air base attack missions during the war included a Nesher or Shahak patrol tasked to cover the retreating attackers if pursued by enemy interceptors. Rarely was the defending patrol vectored deeper into enemy territory to fend off enemy interceptors from fighting the friendly attackers over an enemy air base under attack. Tsalkhiya was only 50km to the rear of the front line in an area where Egyptian SAM battery coverage was less extensive, so a Nesher patrol was

45   The split was 75 Kurnassess (including 62 serviceable), 62 Mirages (61 serviceable), 127 Ahits (117 serviceable), and 17 Saars (all serviceable).

46   Egyptian MiG-17 pilot Hussein Kfass flew six missions from Tsalkhiya from October 6–14. Kfass's missions corresponded well with ILAF monitoring, for example Kfass did not fly on October 9 and 11, the ILAF not monitoring any missions from Tsalkhiya during these days.

ILAF commander Benjamin Peled visited Khatsor on the morning of October 14, where he was photographed in the front passenger seat of Wing 4 commander Amos Lapidoth's car among Squadron 201 Kurnasses, most probably DOG and LAMB, tasked to attack east of Suez Canal Kilometer 87 and 73, respectively, in loft with cluster bombs in support of Command South, which at the time was opposing the Egyptian offensive. (AC)

vectored to Tsalkhiya, engaged the MiG-21s that were intercepting the Ahits, and claimed the shooting down of four MiG-21s.

Kurnass crews reported good hits and many SAM launches during egress, including from the supposedly suppressed Port Said SAM batteries. Ahit pilots evaded the MiG-21s. One ILAF postwar source stated that two MiG-17s were destroyed on the ground and that Tsalkhiya was suppressed for two days. Another ILAF postwar source claimed that one shelter was hit and Tsalkhiya was suppressed for seven days.[47]

47   Egyptian Air Fofrce MiG-17 pilot Hussein Kfass flew only one mission from
      Tsalkhiya in the wake of the ILAF October 14 raid until October 20, and that was
      on October 16, seemingly supporting both ILAF sources.

ILAF Kurnass force attacking Tanta, October 15

BLUE WHITE included refreshment of contingency plans and the refreshed plans were presented to higher echelons. ILAF presented plans to Israel Chief of Staff on April 25, 1973. The principal presenter was ILAF Department Operations Chief Giora Ram. Other ILAF staff officers participated in the presentation as needed or when asked, while ILAF Commander Mordecai Hod opined whenever he felt a clarification was needed. This was normal practice in presentation of plans.

Concerning Operation *Ram*, Ram said:

"Now to air bases. We have two primary plans. There are 26–29 Egyptian air bases depending on definition, what is an active air base. We would like to mess with 20 that can be suppressed in a single wave or we can pick the ten principal air bases – mostly MiG-21 air bases – for destruction. Destruction is 50 percent of the aircraft and damage to the airfield. It will take a long time to repair it, to make it serviceable again. It is 300 bombs dropped on an air base in addition to cluster bombs."

The presentation generated a discussion and it was then that the ILAF Commander remarked:

"I am presenting only a scheme [for an air base destruction raid] because there will be changes, many major changes. I am against 270 bombs [for destruction of an air base in a single raid]. I am pro 500 bombs..."

It was during that discussion that the ILAF Department Operations Chief referred specifically to Tanta and presented the then-ILAF contingency plan for destruction of Tanta: 44 Kurnasses attacking with nearly 400 bombs.

Regardless of ILAF prewar plans to task 44 Kurnasses to a mission aimed at the destruction of Tanta, regardless of the ILAF Commander's aspirations to drop more than 500 bombs to destroy such an air base, the ILAF assigned to the mission to destroy Tanta on October 15 only 28 Kurnasses with just 120 M117 bombs. It was a "mission impossible" right from the start.

Again and again throughout this text, the gap in numbers between ILAF prewar plans for an Operation *Ram* mission aimed at the destruction of an air base and ILAF implementation during the war is presented. At the time of writing there is no known explanation. There may never be.

Day 9, *Ram 8,* Tanta

The ILAF intended to attack Tanta from 1255hrs, but the raid was delayed until 1555hrs. In the meantime, the ILAF monitored eight Tanta Mirages attacking Command South at 1410hrs, while the Egyptian offensive had failed by the time the Israelis raided Tanta.[48]

Operation *Ram 8* targeted Mansura as its secondary target and Tanta as the primary target. Eight Kurnasses were tasked to suppress Mansura and 20 Kurnasses to destroy Tanta. Again, the Kurnass force tasked to destroy Tanta was smaller than specified in the ILAF's prewar plans and was planned to attack with only 90 M117 bombs.[49]

Raiding Mansura was intended to divert defending Egyptian interceptors from Tanta, prevent MiG-21 scrambles from Mansura, and saturate Egyptian Air Force defenses, so H-Hour for raiding Mansura was 20 minutes earlier than that for attacking Tanta. The Mansura attack package included two Kurnasses tasked to loft cluster bombs, with six following Kurnasses tasked to pop with eight bombs per aircraft. The Kurnasses attacked Mansura and immediately afterwards engaged defending MiG-21s. The ILAF claimed that 16 MiG-21s intercepted the eight Kurnasses and credited two Kurnass crews with air-to-air kills, plus that two more MiG-21s were lost during the engagement: one crashed for unknown reasons and another was engaged by an Egyptian SAM in a friendly fire incident. Kurnass crews attacking Mansura are not known to have reported SAM launches, except for observation of some five or six SAMs launched from the Egyptian Air Defense Port Said deployment during egress.

The scramble of four MiG-21s from Mansura was monitored by the ILAF some ten minutes after Mansura was raided. Mansura was evidently not suppressed and the four fresh MiG-21s were probably vectored to intercept the incoming Kurnasses tasked to raid Tanta.

The Tanta attack package was planned to include eight Squadron 119 Kurnasses in two formations and 12 Kurnasses from Squadron 107 in two formations. The Squadron 119 Kurnasses flew the planned route west of Mansura and were not intercepted during ingress, though only the two lead loft crews and three pop crews from the following formation bombed Tanta. Squadron 107 intentionally cut the corner of the planned route, flew much closer to Mansura and was intercepted during ingress. All 12 crews peeled from formation successively to engage the pursuing MiG-21s and none attacked Tanta. The ILAF again recorded 16 MiG-21s, crediting four air-to-air kills to Kurnass crews and claiming that two more MiG-21s crashed during the engagement.

The MiG-21s chased the Kurnasses past the Egyptian coastline so a Nesher patrol was vectored to cover the retreating Kurnasses, but the lead Nesher shot down a Kurnass in a friendly fire incident.

Operation *Ram 8*'s objective to destroy Tanta was not accomplished. The Israeli claim that the Egyptian Air Force lost ten MiG-21s during *Ram 8* may have been slightly optimistic, but nevertheless the claimed destruction of so many combat aircraft was a relatively good result for a *Ram* mission. The objective of the ILAF's *Ram* air base destruction missions was destruction of combat aircraft, and most such missions generated claims of the destruction of far fewer than ten aircraft. Yet regardless of the ten-to-one claims-to-loss ratio, Operation

48   Some 250 Egyptian tanks and about 25 Israeli tanks had been hit during the battle, which started at around 0600hrs and had mostly ended by noon on October 14.

49   The ILAF commander stressed during presentation of plans to the Israeli Defense Force chief on April 25: "I am presenting only a scheme [for an air base destruction raid] because there will be changes, many major changes. I am against 270 bombs [for destruction of an air base in a single raid]. I am pro 500 bombs." (ILGOV Defense Archive)

Ram 8 was yet another ILAF failure to match prewar expectations. The objective of *Ram 8* was the destruction of Tanta, in order to accomplish which the attacking Kurnasses had to destroy at least 15 combat aircraft there through the rendering of at least 15 aircraft shelters unusable. As it happened, just three Kurnasses actually attacked Tanta with M117 bombs and only one shelter may have been damaged.

The Egyptian Air Force probably valued Tanta less than did the ILAF and has since referred to this action as the battle for Mansura. The Egyptian perspective was that the raid had been thwarted, and hence October 14, 1973, became Egyptian Air Force Day.[50]

USAF F-4E 72-131 arriving in Israel on October 14, to become ILAF Kurnass 303. Khatso was the hub for F-4 arrivals since 1969, while Ekron would be the hub for A-4 arrivals – until October 1973, A-4s were shipped from the USA to Israel rather than flown. Wing 4's Squadron 201 escorted incoming F-4s and Air Base 8's Squadron 119 escorted the A-4s. (AC)

Day 9, TOADS

Coinciding with Operation *Ram 8* was the arrival in Israel of nine F-4s. The USA had undertaken to replace ILAF A-4 and F-4 losses as well as to replenish Israeli ordnance stocks. Complexities covering delivery of arms from the USA to Israel during wartime, red tape within US departments, and diplomacy delayed deliveries. Egypt's rejection of a ceasefire accelerated the USA to full power.

The F-4s landed at Khatsor, which had been the ILAF acceptance center for incoming F-4s since 1969. There, they were prepared for ILAF service and allocated to squadrons. Painted in a USAF scheme that was darker than that of the ILAF, repainting was obviously not included in the hasty preparations for Israeli service so the new F-4s – some actually older than Israeli-purchased F-4s – soon earned the informal nickname "toads."

While the toads were landing at Khatsor, C-5 airlifters were already in the air, flying towards Israel. Washington was ensuring that the supposed ILAF order of battle crisis and Israeli ordnance stocks worries would no longer be a problem; the intention was that Israel should now win the war unambiguously so that the other side would seek a ceasefire. The US would be waiting for the call.

50 Sources such as *Osprey Combat Aircraft 44, Arab MiGs* and Wikipedia presented farfetched numbers such as 160 or 250 ILAF A-4s and F-4s fighting 62 Egyptian MiG-21s, while the Egyptian Air Force is presented as having claimed 17 kills versus six or seven losses. The only numbers beyond doubt are 28 Kurnasses tasked to fly the mission and one Kurnass lost; all other numbers are claims and evaluations, some imaginative, some realistic. For example, a realistic evaluation of the number of MiG-21s involved in the action would be 16–32 because the Egyptians vectored two or three four-ship CAPs to intercept the incoming Kurnasses and then scrambled four-ship QRAs from up to three bases: Abu Hammad, Mansura, and Tanta. The presented Egyptian Air Force admission of six or seven losses corresponds well with the ILAF claim for up to ten Egyptian losses

Day 10, *Stouthearted*

The Egyptian offensive played into Israeli hands. The two Egyptian armored divisions had finally crossed the Suez Canal, meaning the rear of the Egyptian armies was now more vulnerable than ever before. Having hit 250 Egyptian tanks within a few hours, the time was ripe for a Command South offensive.

The subsequent Operation *Stouthearted* started with a Command South orders group from 2340hrs on October 14. The 143rd Division would penetrate towards Suez Canal Kilometer 97, between the Egyptian Second Army to the north and the Third Army to the south. Time for boats in the water was set for 1900hrs on October 15. The 143rd Division would then secure a corridor to the crossing point and deploy at least one bridge. The 162nd Division would cross the Suez Canal from 0300hrs on October 16, its prime objective being the destruction of Egyptian SAM batteries. If the 162nd Division tanks could achieve air superiority, the ILAF would be able to support the Israeli Defense Force units west of the Suez Canal while harassing the stranded Egyptian forces east of the waterway.

Concurring with the Command South battle procedure for Operation *Stouthearted* was the first landing in Israel – a minute or so past midnight – of a USAF airlift C-5. The C-5 that landed first was not planned to land first. The C-5 that was supposed to land first was airlifting the USAF air head command party and the specific USAF unloading equipment, but it was delayed along the way so the first C-5 to land delivered 97 tons of artillery ammunition that had to be unloaded with improvised local equipment.

Day 10, *Ram 21*

Qutamiya was some 65km west of Suez Canal Kilometer 145 at the rear of Egypt's Third Army. The ILAF had evaluated that a MiG-17 squadron was based at each of the forward bases Tsalkhiya and Qutamiya, with an obvious mission to support the Second and Third armies. Command South's Operation *Stouthearted* penetration phase was to be fought at night when Egyptian Air Force offensive action was unlikely, but battle was expected to continue on October 16. Suppression of Tsalkhiya and Qutamiya to deny operations from these bases against Command South on October 16 therefore meshed well with Israeli Defense Force plans, though Egypt had more than two squadrons of attack aircraft, including Su-7 squadrons based at Bilbeis to the rear of Tsalkhiya.[51]

The combination of ILAF Air Base 8 Squadron 119 Kurnasses and Squadron 115 Ahits

---

51   For as yet unknown reasons, throughout the October 1973 War the ILAF did
      not attack the Egyptian Bilbeis air base, from where Su-7s operated against
      Command South.

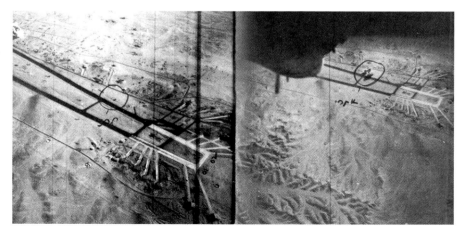

Battle Damage Assessment camera images from a Squadron 107 Kurnass taken on October 15, with a before image to the left and an after image to the right for a hit on some kind of a trench – possibly an AAA emplacement – positioned alongside runway 02/20, with questionable significance for an objective to suppress or destroy an air base. (AC)

had fared well during *Ram 8* against Tsalkhiya, so the same combination plus four Squadron 107 Kurnasses was tasked to raid Qutamiya: four Squadron 119 Kurnasses lofting cluster bombs against AAA, four Squadron 119 Kurnasses popping bombs against runways, 16 Ahits popping bombs at shelters, and four Squadron 107 Kurnasses also popping bombs at shelters.

The ILAF evaluated that Qutamiya was defended by three or four surrounding SAM batteries and monitored the scramble of 20 MiG-21s from five bases. Kurnass crews and Ahit pilots attacked mostly as planned. Cumulative reports indicated the launch of some 20 SAMs that missed the attackers but according to the ILAF hit two MiG-21s from Inchas.

Day 11, *Ram 22*

The ILAF monitored only a single Egyptian Air Force offensive action on October 15, with two Su-7s from Bilbeis attacking Command South east of Suez Canal Kilometer 30. The Israelis documented 161 support sorties along the Command South front line during October 15, with many missions tasked to attack around Suez Canal Kilometer 97 to soften Egyptian targets ahead of *Stouthearted*, though ILAF raids were spread all along the canal to avoid exposure of the sector where *Stouthearted* was planned to take place.

Ram 22 tasked 28 Kurnasses to destroy Tanta. Again, the defending MiG-21 bases of Mansura and Shubra Khit were to be attacked. Four Squadron 69 Kurnasses were tasked to loft cluster bombs at Mansura and Shubra Khit at the same time as H-Hour for attacking Tanta: 1245hrs. The objective was to prevent QRA MiG-21s from taking off because the 28 Kurnasses tasked to attack Tanta were flying along two routes in a pincer attack, with the western route over the Shubra Khit sector and the eastern route over the Mansura sector. Then the two Squadron 69 Kurnasses tasked to loft Mansura were recalled. Perhaps real-time monitoring revealed that attacking Mansura was unnecessary because the Mansura QRA was scrambled prior to H-Hour, as were the MiG-21s QRAs from Abu Hammad, Shubra Khit, and Tanta.

Two Squadron 119 Kurnasses were leading along each route, with the four tasked to loft cluster bombs against AAA, but then not to speed away as usual but to circle Tanta and engage MiG-21s in order to enable the main force to attack as unhindered as possible. The main force included eight Kurnasses from each of Squadron 119, Squadron 201, and Squadron 107 split along the two routes, mostly tasked to aim at aircraft shelters. Like all *Ram* missions, it was supposed to be a massive hit-and-run blow from 1245–1250hrs.

The four loft Kurnasses attacked as planned, but then had to circle cautiously because Tanta was ringed by SAM batteries. Four SAM launches were observed. One SAM hit a Squadron 119 Kurnass prior to its pop-up. The Kurnass turned back but crashed later. While SAMs engaged Kurnasses flying the western route during ingress, MiG-21s intercepted those flying the eastern route during ingress, so Squadron 201 DOG engaged the MiGs while CRAB continued to Tanta.

ILAF Neshers intercepting Egyptian-flown Libyan Mirages

The ILAF rated the Libyan-owned, Egyptian-flown Mirages as the most potent enemy combat aircraft, and they were often mentioned in Israeli discussions concerning preparations for war during April and May 1973, even though there was only one squadron of them based at Tanta. However, the ILAF did not detect any Libyan-owned Egyptian-flown Mirage offensive operations until October 14. Overall, the ILAF monitored seven Tanta Mirage offensive missions covering 29 sorties between October 14 and 22. For comparison, the ILAF Kurnass force, with four squadrons, flew some 3,200 sorties from October 6–24.

Postwar, Libyan leader Gaddafi claimed that the Libyan contribution to the October 1973 War included 400 Mirage sorties, so it is possible that the Tanta Mirages also flew defensive missions that covered more than 300 sorties, which is in line with the ILAF count of Egyptian Air Force activity that yielded some 600 offensive combat aircraft sorties and around 5,500 defensive combat aircraft sorties for a 10–90 percent split between offense and defense.

ILAF Neshers engaged the Tanta Mirages during two of those seven offensive missions. Four Egyptian Mirage interdictor kills were credited during the two engagements – on October 18 and 22 – versus no losses of ILAF Nesher interceptors. Additionally, the Israelis credited a Hawk battery with a Mirage kill.

Prewar ILAF plans figured that 50–60 Kurnasses with ten M117 bombs per aircraft would accomplish destruction of an air base the size of Tanta, but the forces that the ILAF committed to the task on October 14 and 15 were significantly smaller and lifted many fewer bombs than the ILAF's prewar plans had stipulated. This rendered *Ram's* objective to destroy Tanta unrealistic; it was a "mission impossible" right from the start. A Squadron 119 aerial combat scene over Tanta on October 15, as captured by a Kurnass Battle Damage Assessment camera. A MiG-21 that EMPLOYEE 1 had shot down is in the center, the pilot who ejected from the MiG descends under the canopy of his parachute on the right, and another MiG-21 is on the left. (AC)

A MiG-21 crashed while engaging DOG. More MiG-21s intercepted the Kurnasses from the time of their bombing onwards. The ILAF credited a Squadron 119 Kurnass with a MiG-21 kill over Tanta and a Squadron 107 Kurnass with a MiG-21 kill during egress.

The ILAF probably hoped that images from destruction of Tanta would showcase its victory in the October 1973 War, as photographs of destroyed Egyptian aircraft on the ground had represented the ILAF's triumph in the June 1967 War. However, only 18 Kurnasses actually attacked Tanta with just 90 M117 bombs, so again the numbers were too small for the required destruction objective. Tanta was not destroyed. The ILAF again fared well, but not well enough to match its prewar pretensions and as a result once again falling short of Israeli Defense Force expectations.

Day 10–11, Counter crossing

Stouthearted began on October 15. Fierce fighting slowed the 143rd Division; boats hit the water only at around 0130hrs on October 16, more than six hours later than planned. The first Israeli tanks had crossed the Suez Canal over rafts by 0700hrs, but the 143rd Division failed to accomplish the Command South condition for the crossing of the 162nd Division: a bridge across the canal.

The Israelis intercepted an Egyptian Second Army call for fire only at 1040hrs, the Egyptian Air Force responding within less than 30 minutes with strikes against the 143rd Division. *Stouthearted* forced Egypt to commit aerial elements to attack Command South, thereby at last offering ILAF interceptors more opportunities to shoot down Egyptian combat aircraft. The emerging pattern for ILAF action was a main effort to support Command South, including operations to attack Egyptian SAM batteries along the front line, as well as shielding the Command South corridor east of the Suez Canal and the bridgehead west of the Suez Canal from Egyptian aerial attacks.

Still, *Stouthearted* was not wholly successful. The 162nd Division did not cross from 0300hrs on October 16 as planned. Instead, Command South ordered it to accomplish the objective that the 143rd Division had failed to achieve: a bridge across the Suez Canal. The initial momentum had been lost; there would be no swift rush deeper into Egypt. Israeli Defense Force chief was clearly disappointed when he reported to the Prime Minister at 1146hrs: "this is not a situation changing success... we have 28 tanks on the other side [west of the Suez Canal]... there is no bridge... there is a bridgehead... they [Division 143 Brigade 421 tanks] will start to raid SAM batteries... they [Egypt] sent aircraft [to attack the bridgehead] and we shot down three MiGs". [52]

Until the 162nd Division could secure the corridor east of the Suez Canal to enable the deployment of a bridge across the waterway, the 143rd Division bridgehead west of the canal was in a precarious position, primarily due to the inability to supply 421 Brigade's tanks with ammunition and fuel. Meanwhile, until the 162nd Division crossed and started to push forward, 421 Brigade's tanks would raid Egyptian SAM batteries west of the Suez Canal but would have to return to the bridgehead to rearm and refuel. By the end of Day 11, 421 Brigade's tanks had raided several SAM sites and claimed the destruction of two batteries.

52   Postwar, the ILAF credited four kills during that first Egyptian Air Force attack against the Command South bridgehead at around 1145hrs on October 16: one MiG-17 credited to a Squadron 113 Nesher pilot; two MiG-17s credited to Squadron 113 for aircraft that were observed crashing during aerial combat; and one MiG-17 credited to Battalion 208 AAA fire. (ILGOV Defense Archive)

Day 12, ILAF irrelevancy

Until the 162nd Division secured a corridor east of the Suez Canal for safe passage of logistic echelons, Israeli forces counted on the ILAF to supply the 143rd Division. Eight Bell 205 helicopters were tasked to fly a cargo hook mission. A SAM exploded above the lead Bell 205, blast and debris possibly damaging the helicopter, which subsequently turned back. Three more SAMs were then observed and the following helicopters, all intact, also returned to base. At a time when Command South had suffered hundreds of casualties within less than 12 hours during *Stouthearted*, the ILAF helicopters tasked to supply the war-weary 143rd Division and perhaps to evacuate casualties on their way back from the supply mission had turned back.

Forces from Brigade 14, of Command South's Division 143, prior to the start of their advance towards the Suez Canal Kilometer 97 crossing sector on October 15. Within hours, more than half of Brigade 14's tanks would be hit; by the end of the night, it would have suffered more than 120 fatalities and lost more than 50 tanks. (ILGD/A)

The Egyptian response to *Stouthearted* was a classic military action: a pincer attack east of the Suez Canal to cut off the Israeli corridor and a head-on attack west of the canal to destroy the Israeli bridgehead. The pincer attack east of the waterway included a Second Army assault from north to south and a Third Army push from south to north. The Second Army was in contact with Command South throughout *Stouthearted*, while the Third Army was some 30km south of the battlefield. In order to accomplish the southern pincer action, the Third Army attacking force – consisting of 25 Brigade with some 100 T-62 tanks – had to advance along 30km of mostly flat terrain. Command South observations noted that 25 Brigade started moving north from east of Suez Canal Kilometer 130 at around 0720hrs. The Egyptian brigade moved carefully and slowly, giving Command South plenty of time to establish a strong defense. From Command South's perspective, the first force expected to engage the observed enemy was the ILAF, and an initial call for support was issued at 0720hrs. By 0825hrs, Command South observations reported that the enemy force was east of Suez Canal Kilometer 115. Additional requests for ILAF support were issued, one request suggesting the potential to destroy some 200 targets, but there was no Israeli air attack against the southern part of the Egyptian pincer. Command South observations also spotted dozens of armored vehicles east of Suez Canal Kilometer 93, probably an element of the Egyptian Second Army pincer action, but the request for ILAF support was rejected at around 1100hrs.

Throughout this timeframe, Israeli aircraft were attacking Egyptian targets elsewhere, mostly in the Port Said sector at the northern mouth of the Suez Canal and in the Ismailia sector around Suez Canal Kilometer 75, areas that were irrelevant to the main Command South action at that time. Eventually, from 1220hrs, 25 Brigade engaged Command South forces and within hours the Egyptian armored brigade was wiped out.[53]

Day 13, *Cracker 22*

The ILAF's irrelevance during day 12, as well as dashed hopes that Command South would swiftly destroy Egyptian Air Defense elements, possibly prompted the resumption of ILAF operations to suppress and destroy the enemy batteries. Instead of attacking the whole air defense front-line deployment as attempted in Operation *Challenge 4* on October 7, the ILAF changed tactics to attack one sector at a time. The Egyptian Air Defense Port Said sector deployment was already considered destroyed, so the objective of the ILAF's Operation *Cracker 22* was to destroy the front-line sector deployment to the south of Port Said in the Qantara sector, where six Egyptian 107 Brigade SAM batteries had been pinpointed. The Israelis' operational logic

---

53 Wiped out are Shazly's words. Meanwhile, the first Israeli bridge across the Suez Canal was deployed at 1600hrs, and Division 162 planned to cross the canal during the nighttime from the evening of October 17.

Israeli Defense Minister Dayan (right) visited Command South on October 17, where probably sometime after 1000hrs he met Squadron 105 reserve pilot Hanan Tamir (center), who had ejected from his Saar at around 0800hrs. Tamir had been flying as BEERI 3, tasked to attack Egyptian forces north of the Command South corridor to the Suez Canal. He attacked from medium altitude and reported SAM launches, the ILAF attributing BEERI 3's shooting down to a probable SA-6 strike. (ILGP/PO)

was that the destruction of the Port Said SAM batteries opened a supposedly safe corridor for the ingress of the *Cracker 22* attacking force. However, the air defense deployment that *Cracker 22* targeted was around Suez Canal Kilometer 45 in a sector totally irrelevant to Command South operations, which at the time centered around Suez Canal Kilometer 97.

The Israeli Defense Force chief and Command South commander conversed at 0827hrs, apparently agreeing that the ILAF should not attack Egyptian SAM batteries because Command South was fighting well without ILAF support. Nevertheless, *Cracker 22* started at 0930hrs as planned. Within minutes, it was reported that three aircraft had been lost.[54]

Immediately afterwards, the Israeli Defense Minister, who was visiting Command South headquarters at the time, called the Chief of Staff and told him that attacking the Egyptians' Qantara air defense deployment was unnecessary and an error. The Command South commander added that he had specifically told the Israeli Defense Force chief and ILAF commander not to attack Egyptian SAM batteries. The Israeli ground commanders were extremely frustrated because they were fighting without ILAF support in order to preserve the ILAF's numerical strength, yet the ILAF was losing aircraft while attacking in areas irrelevant to the conduct of the war.

Nevertheless, *Cracker 22* continued with additional waves attacking according to plan until 1000hrs. Four Ahits were lost and two were damaged, so ILAF losses during *Cracker 22* amounted to six aircraft, plus three more damaged.

Later that day, the Israeli Defense Force chief summoned the ILAF commander, and among the harsh words that the ground forces officer aimed at the air force officer were:

I am afraid we are not coordinated. I am heading a discussion once a day, lecturing my thoughts for planning the following day's war and you [ILAF] are either absent or partially participating... For example Qantara. Qantara interests my grandmother![55]
The [SAM] batteries [at Qantara] do not bother me. I do not need close air support there... [At Qantara] they do not attack me and I do not attack them [at Qantara]. If it [attacking at Qantara] is good for you [ILAF] then fine. If the by product [of CRACKER 22] is attacking the [Egyptian] forces, the [Egyptian] bridgehead at Qantara, then go ahead but I want to be sure that you [ILAF Commander] understand what interests us, meaning me [IDF Chief].[56]

Later, from 1720hrs, Israeli Defense Minister and the Israel Defence Force deputy chief convened with the Command South commander. The Defense Minister opined again that *Cracker 22* was unnecessary and the Command South commander recommended that the ILAF not attack SAM batteries again in order to minimize ILAF losses, as the ground

54   The report was inaccurate. Three Kurnasses had been hit but only two were lost, the third landing at Refidim.

55   "Interests my grandmother" is Israeli slang meaning that the speaker has absolutely no interest in the discussed subject.

56   Throughout the war, the Israeli Defense Force accepted the ILAF's independent operations that seemingly served Israeli objectives to hit the enemy wherever possible, with the resulting damage hopefully contributing to winning the war, yet tolerance of this independent action seems to have eroded due to ILAF losses, the inability to fulfill prewar presumptions, and shortcomings in meeting the ground forces' air support expectations. (ILGOV Defense Archive)

forces would continue to destroy SAM batteries to enable ILAF support. The Israeli Deputy Chief of Staff indicated that the ILAF was also tasked to supply the Command South bridgehead west of the Suez Canal, but by that time a second bridge was being towed towards the canal, the corridor had been secured, and an ILAF attempt to supply the bridgehead had failed, so the Command South commander concluded that the bridgehead would not count on the ILAF, with supplies pushed forward through the corridor and across the bridges.[57]

The Israeli Defense Force chief visited the ILAF Command Post from 1900hrs to make sure that the two organizations were working in unison, stressing that the plan for the following day included a Command South offensive against Egyptian air defenses plus ILAF support to Command South in sectors that had been cleared from SAM batteries.

The ILAF therefore forwarded a plan for Day 14 that included the following:

- Squadron 102 Ahits would operate over the Port Said sector.
- Squadron 109 and 110 Ahits would operate over the Qantara sector.
- Squadron 105 Saars and Squadron 116 Ahits would support the Command South bridgehead.
- Squadron 115 Ahits would operate over the sector south of the bridgehead, attacking in loft profile since that sector had not been cleared of SAM batteries.
- The Kurnass force would fly Shrike patrols and chaff screening as well as missions against the enemy's rear.
- The Mirage squadrons would continue to focus on air-to-air combat missions.

Later on October 17, Israeli Defense Minister Dayan (left) visited Command South's Division 143, where he met its commander Sharon (second from left) and Brigade 14 commander Reshef (front right, wearing a protective vest) at around 1600hrs east of Suez Canal Kilometer 100, near Fort Sweettooth. Destroyed Egyptian SA-2 missiles in the background evidently prove that Egypt did deploy SAM batteries on the east bank of the Suez Canal. (ILGD/A)

Day 14, ILAF suffers no losses

The ILAF internalized the Israel Defense Force's criticism: there would be no major operations against Egyptian air defense or air units on October 19. The ILAF's air base attack campaign had practically finished. It had raided 19 Egyptian and Syrian air bases between October 7 and 18, but not one was destroyed. Only seven aircraft were claimed hit on the ground and only some 30 shelters were claimed to have been hit, a ratio of one single, significant, claimed hit per 100 or so bombs. Additionally, the ILAF claimed to have shot down some 30 Egyptian and Syrian air force aircraft during the air base campaign. The Israelis flew some 550 air base attack sorties and lost eight Kurnasses. The overall exchange ratio of the air base campaign from October 7–18 was, at best, one loss per eight gains; an acceptable exchange ratio for an air superiority campaign, but the impact upon the conduct of war was abysmal. Neither the

57 The second Command South bridge across the Suez Canal was reported in the water at 1830hrs.

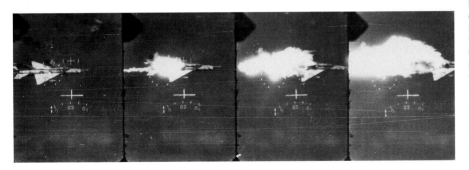

Egyptian Air Force attacks against the Command South bridgehead west of the Suez Canal prompted aerial combat and generated some iconic ILAF air-to-air images, such as this one. ILAF Squadron 101 Nesher pilot Gideon Livni shooting down a MiG-21 over the Command South bridgehead at around 1600hrs on October 18. (AC)

EVENTS

The ILAF sliced the frontline Egyptian SAM deployment into sectors: E-21 F-26 F-27 F-24 F-36 F-35.

The sectors were coded by letters from north to south. ILAF assigned each SAM battery site with a prefix letter denoting the sector and a number identifier. Sector F was from Suez Canal Kilometer 44 down south to Suez Canal Kilometer 57, and ILAF had pinpointed at least 19 SAM sites within the sector F strip up to 30km west of the Suez Canal. The pinpointed SAM sites were the only sites that had been prepared for SA-2 or SA-3 batteries while SA-6 batteries could deploy almost anywhere and had to be constantly monitored for pinpointing.

1. Operation *Cracker 22* targeted three SA-2 batteries E-21, F-24 and F-36 plus three SA-3 batteries F-26, F-27 and F-35. Each battery was to be attacked by three pairs in quick succession: a Kurnass pair, an Ahit H pair and an Ahit E pair. The approach was at the lowest altitude possible from north to south, the attack pattern was a modified pop with a zoom to 12,000ft for more time to acquire the target, then bombing in dive with minimum altitude set at 4,500ft to minimize risk from AAA and SA-7 then turning east for egress at the shortest route.

2. Minutes before H-Hour Squadron 110 Ahit E pilots and Squadron 201 Kurnass crews, flying from east to west, engaged the targeted SAM batteries with Shrikes.

3. Squadron 119 Kurnasses penetrated in between Tsalkhiya to the west and the SAM batteries to the east were tasked to release chaff that would hopefully drift east to screen the attackers.

4. Throughout the operation, helicopters flew east of the Suez Canal tasked to jam radars.

Operation *Cracker 22*, SAM destruction in Egypt, Qantara sector

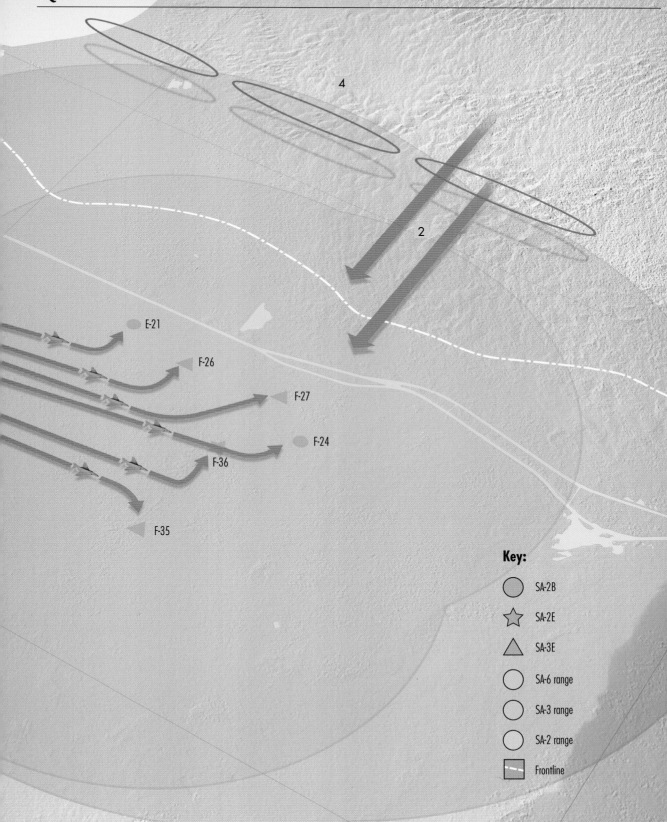

4

2

E-21

F-26

F-27

F-24

F-36

F-35

Key:

⬤ SA-2B

☆ SA-2E

△ SA-3E

◯ SA-6 range

◯ SA-3 range

◯ SA-2 range

▭ Frontline

Egyptian nor the Syrian air forces had been destroyed, so the ILAF failed to accomplish the preset Israeli objective: the destruction of enemy forces. Overall, the impact of the air base attack campaign was hardly noticeable; the ILAF counted more than 1,100 Egyptian and Syrian combat aircraft sorties on October 6 and 7, and some 1,300 on October 18 and 19.

The ILAF's perceived alternative to the failed air base attack campaign was an air-to-air campaign aimed at accomplishing destruction of the Egyptian fighter force. Signaling the shift, Israel's Defense Minister reported to the Israeli Prime Minister that the ILAF had lost 100 combat aircraft out of an initial inventory of 300, that the ground forces were doing well without air support, and that the ILAF should focus on air-to-air combats that had generated a ratio of 15 kills per one Israeli loss.

The ILAF had a marked air-to-air combat capability advantage, so the Egyptian and Syrian air forces mostly limited such actions to engagements over the front lines when the ILAF intercepted air attacks or to combats over Egypt's and Syria's rear areas when their aircraft intercepted ILAF raids. The ILAF's deliberate attempts to draw the Egyptian and Syrian air forces into aerial combats over closer and safer zones such as the Mediterranean Sea and the Red Sea, through bombing of targets such as radar stations, mostly failed.

Israeli ground counteroffensives triggered Egypt and Syria to fly more air support missions over the front lines, so air-to-air warfare indeed intensified along the timeline of the war and the ILAF was doing well in air-to-air combat. The postwar ILAF official numbers were 237 combat aircraft kills from October 6–18, for the loss of 14 Israeli combat aircraft, a ratio of 17 kills per loss. However, at an average of 18 combat aircraft air-to-air kills per day, it would have taken the ILAF approximately a month of fighting to destroy the remaining Egyptian and Syrian fighter forces from October 19 onwards.

Time was running out. The USSR started pressing hard for a ceasefire; US support for Israel was clearly outweighing Soviet airlifts to Egypt and Syria. Iraqi and Jordanian expeditionary forces stabilized Syria's stance, but the initial Syrian gains had been lost. Egypt was no longer in possession of both banks of the Suez Canal. The side that had imposed the war upon Israel on October 6, the side that had objected to the Israeli proposition from October 12 to end the war, was seemingly seeking a ceasefire. Regardless of Israeli Defense Force deficiencies and ILAF failures, Israel was doing just fine.

Day 15, *Cracker 23*

Israel's Prime Minister asked the Israeli Defense Force chief how much time was needed to finish the war satisfactorily from their perspective. At least three days was his answer. The USA consequently notified the USSR that Secretary of State Henry Kissinger would travel to Moscow to negotiate in person the Soviet demand for a ceasefire in the Middle East. Within two hours, the Prime Minister informed the Defense Minister that Israeli forces had got the requested three more days of fighting.

Day 14 of the war, October 19, was a positive one for the ILAF, which claimed the destruction of 27 enemy aircraft for no losses of its own. The Egyptian front line was seemingly clear of SAMs from Suez Canal Kilometer 45 northwards, where the ILAF attacked by dive bombing as well as dropping optically guided precision munitions that were not viable for operations over SAM-defended zones. Kurnasses from Squadron 119 attacked with GBU-8s, claiming the destruction of two radars in the Port Said sector as well as hits on three tanks. Ahits of Squadron 116 attacked with AGM-62s and claimed to have hit three tanks. South of Suez Canal Kilometer 45, the ILAF operated mostly in loft and pop, with massive screening from Kurnasses flying

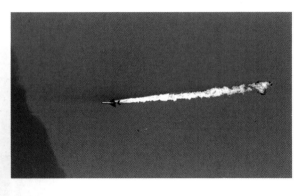

A MiG-21 over Command South forces at around 1330hrs on October 19, after the pilot had ejected. At the time, the ILAF reported the shooting down of 11 Egyptian aircraft, while postwar it claimed 12 kills. (ILGP/PO)

Kurnass 320 – USAF F-4E 71-246 – was the only Operation *Commando* "toad" issued to Squadron 107 during the October 1973 War. It was ferried from Khatsor to Khatserim at noon on October 20, tested late afternoon the same day, thereafter flying four missions until the end of the war. (AC)

Shrike patrols, Kurnasses dispensing chaff, and helicopters flying stand-off jamming missions.

The ILAF forecasted 264 combat aircraft ready for operations on the morning of October 20, and its plans for Day 15 were as follows:

- Destruction of Egyptian SAM batteries in the Ismailia sector in order to clear the front line of missile sites south to Suez Canal Kilometer 80.
- Attacking the SAM batteries defending Egypt's air base at Qutamiya to enable the ILAF to interdict along the Cairo Suez highway, Command South code DARNING.
- Squadron 69 Kurnasses to attack with AGM-65 missiles in the Qantara sector around Suez Canal Kilometer 45.[58]
- Squadron 102 Ahits to bomb in the Port Said sector.
- Squadron 109 and 110 Ahits to bomb in the Qantara sector.
- Squadron 105 Saars and Squadron 116 Ahits to support the Command South bridgehead west of the Suez Canal.
- Squadron 115 Ahits to attack in loft south of the Command South bridgehead where Egyptian SAM batteries were still operational.
- Kurnass crews to fly Shrike patrols during Israeli bombings and support missions.
- Kurnass crews and Mirage pilots to patrol to defend Israeli forces from enemy air raids.
- Airlifters to stand ready to drop supplies to the Command South bridgehead west of the Suez Canal or to fly supplies to Fayid if Command South attacked and secured that Egyptian air base west of Suez Canal Kilometer 107, some 10km south of the Command South bridges across the Suez Canal and with prospects for safe inbound/outbound approaches over Lake Bitter.

H-Hour for Operation *Cracker 23* was 0855hrs. The objective was the destruction of Egypt's SAM batteries in the Ismailia sector, where the ILAF had pinpointed only three remaining batteries: two SA-3s and one SA-2. Lessons learned from *Cracker 22* were implemented in planning for *Cracker 23*; targets were approached from within the screen of support measures, with bombing from medium altitude. The small number of targets enabled the tasking of only Kurnasses to attack the SAM batteries. Eight Squadron 107 Kurnasses attacked two batteries, while four Squadron 119 Kurnasses bombed the remaining battery. The Israelis claimed all three batteries destroyed. As a follow-up, four Squadron 119 Kurnasses were tasked to attack a SAM battery west of Fayid at 0910hrs; the target battery was empty, but an adjacent SAM site was active so the first two Kurnasses attacked the target battery and the trailing two Kurnasses bombed the occupied SAM site, both of which were claimed as destroyed.

The action against the Qutamiya SAM batteries was less successful. Two waves were planned. In the first wave, Squadron 69 attacked and lost a Kurnass, attributed to an SA-6 hit. The second wave, involving Squadron 201, was therefore canceled and the Kurnass crews already in the air were retasked to bomb armored units in an location that Command

---

58   The AGM-65 was a new weapon in the ILAF's inventory, having been flown to Israel in the US airlift.

Kurnass Battle Damage Assessment camera image of Fayid during an air support mission at around 1300hrs on October 20. The black dots along runway 09/27 and the narrower parallel taxiway may have been sabotage craters to prevent potential ILAF operations from Fayid, which is visible in this image showing the Sweet Water Canal at the bottom of the frame beside the northern part of Fayid town. (AC)

South called Missouri to the north of the Israeli corridor from where Egyptian Second Army artillery was bombarding the Israeli bridges across the Suez Canal. The Squadron 201 crews reported bombing mostly vehicles, not armor or artillery. The launch of a single SA-2 missile was observed over a sector that the ILAF had supposedly cleared of Egyptian SAM batteries.

Israel's Division 252 also crossed the Suez Canal and was tasked to invade Fayid. Kurnasses from Squadrons 69 and 107 bombed the large British-built barracks adjacent to the airfield. Yasur helicopters were tasked to land Israeli troops at Fayid. The ILAF monitored the scramble of Egyptian MiG-21s from Inchas and Mansura, which were vectored to Fayid, probably tasked to intercept the Israeli helicopters. The Egyptians also launched several SAMs that according to the ILAF downed a MiG-21 and damaged a Yasur, again over a sector that the ILAF had supposedly cleared of SAM batteries.[59]

Egyptian forces defending Fayid repelled the Israeli heliborne assault, so the capture of the airfield would have to wait for the advance of Division 252 tanks. Meanwhile, Division 162 was advancing south in a sector west of Division 252 and reported a huge amount of Egyptian military traffic along DARNING, mostly moving west from Suez City in the direction of Cairo. Within less than an hour, Squadron 115 Ahits bombed vehicles along DARNING regardless of the ILAF's evaluation that the Egyptian Air Defense Qutamiya deployment had not been destroyed.[60]

The ILAF daily report to the Israel Defense Force was true to 1600hrs. The report for October 20 included the claimed destruction of only three enemy aircraft – two Egyptian and one Syrian – to highlight a weakness in the ILAF's shift from an air campaign against air bases that was wholly dependent upon the action of ILAF, to an air-to-air campaign that was dependent upon Egyptian and Syrian aerial forces' levels of activity as well as their willingness to engage Israeli aircraft in combat. Luckily for the ILAF, Egyptian Air Force elements attacked the Command South bridgehead and corridor around 1630hrs. Israel claimed the shooting down of ten Egyptian combat aircraft during Day 15, but a Nesher was lost during the afternoon and another Kurnass was lost around sunset; the end of Day 15 exchange ratio in air warfare was thus three Israeli losses versus 11 ILAF claims for destruction of enemy aircraft.[61]

Day 16, *Dessert*
ILAF plans for October 21 mostly mirrored those for Day 15, except for a change of main mission for the four Kurnass squadrons from attacking the enemy's rear and high-value targets to supporting Command South.

Israel's Defense Minister pressed for swifter Command South action in order to maximize the gaining of ground west of the Suez Canal within the shortest possible

59　Likewise two Kurnass formations reported the launch of SAMs: Squadron 201's LIONCUB, tasked to mine west of Port Said at 1400hrs, reported three SA-2 launches from somewhere between Ismailia and Qantara, while Squadron 119's STEEPLEJACK, tasked to bomb Fayid camps at 1415hrs, reported the launch of three SA-2s. STEEPLEJACK did not indicate from where the SA-2s were launched, so it is possible that the two reports referred to a single action.

60　Four 115 Squadron Ahit pilots attacking DARNING 68 – some 35km west of the Suez Canal – at 1410hrs reported AAA fire from a point coded Red 5119, some 5km north of DARNING 70, but no SAM launches.

61　The ILAF's official postwar claim for day 15 was 15 kills plus the shooting down of four AS-5 air-to-ground missiles that had been launched by Egyptian Tu-16s.

timeframe, but Division 143's failure to comply with *Stouthearted* time targets enabled Egypt to stiffen its defense west of the Suez Canal so Division 162's thrust was slower than the minister's expectations. By noon, the 162nd Division reported the destruction of 21 SAM batteries and the ILAF's bombing campaign aimed at the Egyptian front-line forces was intensifying, but the 162nd Division was still far from accomplishing the encirclement of Egypt's Third Army, while Egyptian defense and terrain difficulties prevented the 143rd Division from advancing north to encircle the Egyptian Second Army.

An Israeli soldier examines a MiG-17 – possibly a dummy – at Fayid. Egyptian combat aircraft are not known to have operated from Fayid during the October 1973 War, but helicopters probably did and the air base had shelters for aircraft, so perhaps the Egyptian Air Force planned to deploy combat aircraft to Fayid if an offensive deeper into Sinai had succeeded. (ILGD/A Bamakhaneh (in *Camp IDF Magazine*))

Expecting pressure from the USSR to result in a ceasefire, Operation *Dessert* was aimed at repossession of the Mount Hermon fort, the only remaining Syrian territorial gain. The ILAF was tasked to bomb Syrian strongpoints atop Mount Hermon, to patrol over Mount Hermon in order to prevent Syrian aerial support for the Syrian forces at Mount Hermon, and to airlift 317 Brigade that was tasked to capture part of the Syrian side of the Mount Hermon ridge to the north of the Israeli fort that 1 Brigade was tasked to retake in an uphill frontal assault from south to north.

Five Yasur helicopters initiated the airlift from around 1400hrs, a sixth joining within an hour after some 200 troops had been airlifted. After 1600hrs, when the Yasurs had airlifted more than 400 troops to the Syrian side of Hermon ridge, Syria countered with Mi-8 helicopters and tanks tasked to climb from Arna at 1,500m altitude to the 2,381m-altitude Syrian fort along some 10km of mostly exposed track. Israeli artillery and ILAF interceptors blocked both efforts, reporting the destruction of two Mi-8 helicopters and claiming the shooting down of two MiG-21s.

Day 17, Ceasefire

Brigade 317 captured the Syrian Mount Hermon fort after midnight and ended Operation *Dessert* with two fatalities, while Brigade 1 recaptured the Israeli Mount Hermon fort at a cost of more than 50 fatalities. In between completion of the two brigades' missions, the USA and USSR's mutually agreed ceasefire initiative evolved at 0652hrs into a UN call for an end to the fighting within 12 hours. Washington and the Israeli government had given the Israel Defense Force the three days that the Chief of Staff had requested, but while Command North had completed the recapture of Mount Hermon on time, Command South had been ignoring the Defense Minister's urging to speed up the action and was clearly behind schedule to accomplish even a Pyrrhic victory.[62]

Command South finally ordered the 162nd and 252nd Division to speed up their advance to the southern mouth of the Suez Canal to trap the Egyptian Third Army. The 162nd Division's artillery has been suppressing the remaining SAM batteries and the ILAF had intensified its bombing, but most missions were attack rather than support and many targets were rear echelons rather than front-line forces.

The Egyptian Air Force responded to the intensified Israeli action by attacking Command South at 1030hrs and again at 1600hrs in support of the Egyptian effort to limit Israeli gains

62 Command South had been unable to destroy the Egyptian forces along the front line so Operation *Stouthearted* was aimed at an alternative victory that included larger territorial gains and a blockade that would threaten to annihilate at least part of the Egyptian front-line forces, but neither element of the alternative victory scheme was accomplished by the time the UN called for a ceasefire.

A MiG-17 over the Golan Heights, possibly on October 21, when at around 1540hrs, in the Mount Hermon sector, ILAF Kurnasses engaged MiG-17s and MiG-21s that were reported as being bare metal/silver, leading the ILAF to figure that these could have been attrition replacement aircraft since Syrian MiGs were usually in camouflage schemes. [ILGD/A Bamakhaneh (in *Camp* IDF Magazine), photographer Uzi Keren)

west of the Suez Canal while holding on to the Second and Third armies' bridgeheads east of the canal.

Syrian Air Force elements attacked Command North forces in the Mount Hermon sector at noon, possibly fearing that the Israeli action there was also aimed at an expansion of Israeli territorial gains prior to the ceasefire.

The Israeli Defense Force's chief of staff and intelligence chief, along with the ILAF commander, briefed US Secretary of State Kissinger about the military situation from 1615hrs. Kissinger had landed in Israel at around 1200hrs on his way back from Moscow to Washington. The ILAF commander reported that Egypt's front-line air defense deployment had been destroyed, that Syria was still fielding 16 or 17 SAM batteries across the front line, and that Egypt and Syria had lost 459 aircraft at the cost of 105 Israeli aircraft.[63]

Shortly after the briefing started, the Israeli intelligence chief informed the participants that two Soviet MiG-25s had departed Cairo West and were flying over the front line, presumably on a photographic mission, possibly signaling to Israel that the USSR was backing the Egyptian consent for a ceasefire. Israel was unimpressed. Command South was ordered to stop firing but to continue its advance. If Egyptian forces fired at the advancing Israelis then Command South was authorized to return fire. Egypt had decided when to start the war. Israel wanted to decide when to end it.[64]

Day 18, No ceasefire yet

Egypt accepted the ceasefire. Syria did not. Israel wished to continue fighting Egypt but to stop fighting Syria. The initial Israeli plan for October 23 was a probable ceasefire in the south and expected fighting in the north. Israeli intelligence indicated that a combined Iraqi, Jordanian, and Syrian offensive would start around dawn, so the ILAF plan for Day 18 was to attack Syria's remaining SAM batteries while supporting Command North with loft missions at least until the effectiveness of attacking the SAM batteries could be ascertained. Additionally, the Israeli

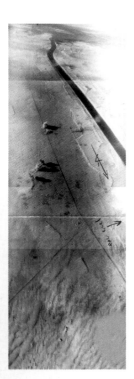

63   The Egyptian Air Defense's front-line deployment was indeed severely battered, but probably not totally destroyed. At least five ILAF formations attacking Egyptian forces around the time of the briefing reported SAM launches. The ILAF commander presented to Kissinger the following alleged breakdown of Egyptian and Syrian aircraft losses:
Egypt: 113 MiG-21s, 49 MiG-17s, 35 Su-7s, four Su-20s, seven Hunters, three Mirages, one Tu-16, 33 Mi-8s, and nine L-29s.
Syria: 100 MiG-21s, 47 MiG-17s, 37 Su-7s, nine Su-20s, and 12 Mi-8s.
The ILAF end-of-day report indicated no losses on October 22, while ILAF losses from the start of war comprised 32 Kurnasses, 53 Ahits, 11 Mirages, and six Saars, plus two helicopters and two light aircraft.

64   Israel actually had a green light from the USA. Earlier that day, Dayan asked Kissinger "So what should we do? I'd not like to stop [fighting Egypt]." Kissinger answered "That's in your domestic jurisdiction... I'll be on an airplane [flying from Israel to USA]. Just say you'll stop at 1800, provided they do. What we're communicating to the Russians is that we've been informed you'll stop [firing] at 1800 provided they [the Egyptians] stop." (FRUS)
The US backing for Israel throughout the war was categorical, its objective an unequivocal Israeli victory that would force Egypt to abandon the USSR and turn to the USA in order to accomplish the Egyptian objective to repossess Sinai, this time through a US-mediated peace process.

government approved an Israeli Defense Force request to bomb a fuel storage complex north of Damascus in order to signal to Syria that the continuation of hostilities would result in extensive damage deep inside its borders.

The initial ILAF plan for October 23 did not include any offensive action in the south, but as expected the Israeli advance policy generated Egyptian fire. An Israeli Defense Force spokesperson stated at 0035hrs that Egyptian forces had been firing at Israeli forces. The ceasefire was thus off in the south as well.

The ILAF reported the availability of 304 combat aircraft, including 264 serviceable, at 0600hrs, and started supporting Command North at around that time. Within an hour, the ILAF was also ordered to support Command South; the first missions were flown after 0800hrs, mostly aimed at static Egyptian Third Army targets including armor, bombing from medium altitude against the diminishing threat from Egyptian SAM batteries but with comprehensive support from stand-off jammers, chaff clouds, and Shrike patrols.

Kurnass crews raided Syrian POL facilities around 1015hrs with massive Mirage participation, the ILAF objective being to draw the Syrian Air Force into combat and to shoot down many MiGs, on top of the wider Israeli objective to signal to Syria that accepting a ceasefire would be wiser than to continue fighting. Syrian MiG-21s indeed intercepted the Israelis. The ILAF claimed ten kills in the ensuing aerial combat, postwar slightly scaling down the claim to nine, crediting Kurnass crews with four kills and Mirage pilots with five.

Syrian combat aircraft flew nearly 300 defensive sorties on October 23 but did not fly offensive missions over the front line. Egyptian aerial elements also continued to focus on defense during Day 18, but around 1130hrs the ILAF monitored the departure of four MiG-17s from Qutamiya in what appears to be the only Egyptian combat aircraft offensive action that day. Patrolling Mirages were vectored to intercept the MiG-17s, while Egypt vectored MiG-21s to face the incoming Mirages. The ILAF claimed three MiG-21s and two MiG-17s shot down, with one Mirage damaged but landing at Fayid.[65]

The ILAF end-of-day claim was 21 aircraft shot down – 11 in the south and ten in the north – while flying nearly 600 combat aircraft sorties, including 370 offensive sorties mostly in the south, without suffering any losses.[66]

Syria acceded to the ceasefire initiative with a vague statement at 1815hrs. Around that time, Command South's 162nd Division reached DARNING, the Cairo–Suez highway. The 252nd Division then passed through the 162nd Division and approached the coast of the Gulf of Suez south of Adabiya, south of Suez City, around 2300hrs to practically accomplish the encirclement of the Egyptian Third Army.

65 Command South had invaded the Egyptian air base at Fayid, west of Suez Canal Kilometer 107, and after the surrounding perimeter was secured the airfield became a major hub for Command South medical and logistic operations, with ILAF helicopters evacuating casualties from front lines to a field hospital at Fayid and airlifters flying in supplies and troops and flying out casualties to hospitals in Israel after initial medical treatment in the field hospital at Fayid.

66 Postwar, the ILAF credited 18 kills on October 23: nine in the north and nine in the south. In addition to the damaged Nesher that landed at Fayid, two Kurnasses were damaged during support missions and landed at Refidim, while a Syrian MiG-21 hit a Shahak with an AA-2 Atoll air-to-air missile but the damaged Shahak returned to base Ramat David.

By the time US Secretary of State Henry Kissinger landed at Israel's Lod International Airport at around noon on October 22, – when this image was taken – the USAF airlift to Israel had switched from landing in Israel during nighttime to landings during day and night. The USAF coded the airlift to Israel Operation *Nickel Grass* and recorded 567 missions – 145 C-5s and 422 C-141s – that flew 22,318 tons along the 10,000km route, demonstrating US superiority over the USSR, whose An-12s and An-22s had airlifted 15,000 tons in 935 missions over a 3,000km route. (ILGP/PO)

OPPOSITE
An ILAF Squadron 201 Kurnass bombing Egyptian Second Army forces along Route Lexicon at around 0730hrs on October 22. The view is from north (bottom) to south (top), with five bombs at the lower left corner of the frame, the Suez Canal's east bank on the left, the west bank on the right, Ismailia at the top, and the Firdan bridge to the right of the Route Lexicon and Route Khaviva junction. The visible sector of the Suez Canal is from roughly Kilometer 70 to 77. (AC)

OPPOSITE ILAF ATTACKS ON OCTOBER 24, 1973

These attacks primarily targeted Egypt's Third Army in the southern sector of the front.

Day 19, Ceasefire

After all three warring nations accepted the UN call, a ceasefire was set for 0700hrs on October 24. The Israeli Defense Force plan for Day 19 of the war was minimal action in the north versus Iraqi, Jordanian, and Syrian forces, but maximum effort in the south against Egypt.

The ILAF assigned Mirages for air-to-air missions, but did not plan offensive operations for October 24, so the Kurnass force would be tasked to attack along the Command South front line, mostly in the southern sector where the Egyptian Third Army was being encircled. Half an Ahit squadron was assigned to support Command North, whereas five-and-a-half Ahit and Saar squadrons were assigned to support Command South. [67]

The ILAF aspired to maximize attacks against the Egyptian Third Army prior to 0700hrs, but the weather – morning mists – impacted attack and support operations that indeed ended at 0700hrs. However, fighting persisted past the time set for the ceasefire; Israeli attack and support missions were resumed around 1100hrs, and the ILAF commander reported at 1240hrs that some 80 attack and support sorties had been flown after 0700hrs, with no observations of Egyptian SAM launches and no losses.

Shortly afterwards, Egyptian MiG-21s appeared over the battlefield. The Israelis vectored 12 Mirages to the engagement zone, initially reporting the shooting down of 16 MiG-21s.[68]

ILAF attack and support missions continued until sunset at around 1700hrs, flying some 300 air-to-ground sorties, mostly against the Third Army. Although the ILAF did not lose any combat aircraft during Day 19, a Yasur helicopter flying a casualty evacuation mission crashed around 1530hrs some 20km west of Suez Canal Kilometer 145, the ILAF's last loss in the October 1973 War.

ILAF Squadron 101 Shahak sight images from air combat over Syria at around 1015hrs on October 23, with pilot Israel Baharav – at the time Squadron 101's acting commander – acquiring a MiG-21 over a town, as presented in the frame on the left, and firing at it several times until the MiG pilot ejected, as captured in the frame on the right. (AC)

67 Squadron 109 was divided between Command North and Command South. Ahits from Squadron 102 and Saars from Squadron 105 were assigned to the Suez City sector west of Suez Canal Kilometer 160, with half of Squadron 109 and Squadron 110 assigned to support east of the Suez Canal, from Suez Canal Kilometer 135 in the north to Suez Canal Kilometer 160 in the south. Meanwhile, Squadron 115 and Squadron 116 were assigned to support along DARNING from Suez to Cairo. All ILAF support for Command South was planned over the southern sector of the front against Egypt's Third Army, where the Egyptian SAM deployment had been mostly destroyed.

68 Later that day, the number was amended to 15. The postwar ILAF claim for Day 19 was 14 kills. Later the ILAF was credited with 11 kills on October 24.

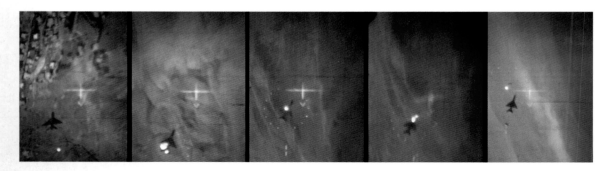

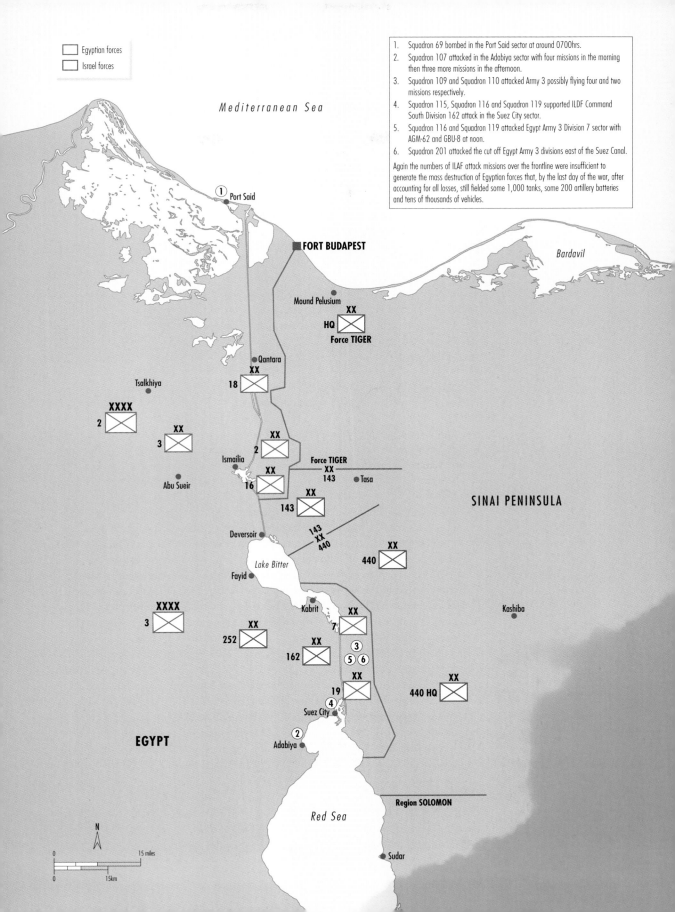

Egyptian forces

Israel forces

Mediterranean Sea

1. Squadron 69 bombed in the Port Said sector at around 0700hrs.
2. Squadron 107 attacked in the Adabiya sector with four missions in the morning then three more missions in the afternoon.
3. Squadron 109 and Squadron 110 attacked Army 3 possibly flying four and two missions respectively.
4. Squadron 115, Squadron 116 and Squadron 119 supported ILDF Command South Division 162 attack in the Suez City sector.
5. Squadron 116 and Squadron 119 attacked Egypt Army 3 Division 7 sector with AGM-62 and GBU-8 at noon.
6. Squadron 201 attacked the cut off Egypt Army 3 divisions east of the Suez Canal.

Again the numbers of ILAF attack missions over the frontline were insufficient to generate the mass destruction of Egyptian forces that, by the last day of the war, after accounting for all losses, still fielded some 1,000 tanks, some 200 artillery batteries and tens of thousands of vehicles.

① Port Said

FORT BUDAPEST

Bardavil

Mound Pelusium

HQ — XX — Force TIGER

Qantara

XX — 18

Tsalkhiya

XXXX — 2

XX — 3

Ismailia

XX — 2

Force TIGER — XX — 143 — Tasa

Abu Sueir

XX — 16

143

XX — 143

SINAI PENINSULA

Deversoir

143 — XX — 440

Lake Bitter

XX — 440

Fayid

Kashiba

XXXX — 3

Kabrit

XX — 7

XX — 252

XX — 162

③
⑤ ⑥

XX — 19

④

Suez City

XX — 440 HQ

② Adabiya

EGYPT

Red Sea

Region SOLOMON

N

0 ___ 15 miles
0 ___ 15km

Sudar

ANALYSIS AND AFTERMATH

Empty SA-2 launcher in one of the more than 50 Egyptian Air Defense SAM sites that had been overrun by Command South, west of the Suez Canal. (ILGP/PO)

The start of the October 1973 War saw an offensive-oriented force – ILAF – supporting a defensive battle against defensive-oriented forces – the Egyptian and Syrian Air Defenses and Egyptian and Syrian Air Forces – participating in an offensive ground campaign. The anomaly was not coincidental, for all these Egyptian and Syrian forces had been restructured to defend against the ILAF's offensive potential.

The ILAF started the war on the defensive, but from the second day of the conflict the war in the air changed, the ILAF operating mostly offensively against the mostly defensive air forces and air defenses of Egypt and Syria.

Egypt's and Syria's aerial forces and air defenses therefore fought mostly in line with prewar plans, which is the preferred path to wage a war and has in many cases generated the greatest victories. The ILAF, on the other hand, had to acknowledge that prewar plans – at least those that were implemented – were failing and to adapt to the evolving reality along the timeline of the war.

The October 1973 War actually encompassed several air campaigns. The prominent air campaigns were ILAF offensives:

- An air campaign aimed at accomplishment of air superiority or even air supremacy over the battlefields that were mostly defended by Egyptian and Syrian air defenses.
- An air campaign aimed at destruction of the air forces of Egypt and Syria.
- An air campaign to support the Israeli Defense Force.
- An air campaign – Operation *Dominique* – that targeted infrastructure, mostly deeper in the enemy's rear, with an objective to impose upon the enemy leadership a decision to end the war.
- An air-to-air campaign that except for – mostly failed – ILAF missions aimed at drawing the Egyptian and Syrian air forces into large-scale air combats was not a standalone air campaign yet deserves a separate analysis.

ILAF air campaign to destroy Egyptian Air Defense and Syrian Air Defense

SAMs have been the ILAF's nemesis since 1970, when the deployment of a Soviet air defense division to Egypt and the subsequent shooting down of five Kurnasses seemed to have eroded ILAF aspirations for air superiority over battlefields. The ILAF experienced attacking SAM batteries in pod formation during 1970 and with anti-radiation missiles in 1971, but then planned large-scale operations aimed at destruction of the whole front-line air defense deployments of Egypt or Syria within a day or a wave, respectively. The plan was to suppress AAA in loft and to destroy SAM batteries in pop, with the support of chaff, decoys, and jamming.

Before the war, the ILAF emphasized that an operation aimed at destruction of Egyptian or Syrian air defense units should precede an Israeli Defense Force offensive. The Israelis' original plan on October 6 was destruction of the Syrian air defense on October 7 ahead of a Command North offensive on October 8. The first two ILAF air superiority operations against Egyptian and Syrian air defense elements on October 7 – Operation *Challenge 4* and Operation *Model 5* – were not in the context of an Israeli Defense Force offensive. The operations were aimed to destroy the whole front-line deployments of Egyptian and Syrian SAM batteries to enable unlimited ILAF support to Command South and Command North, but calls for support were limited in place and time, not spread all along the front lines, and not in demand all the time. *Challenge 4* was called off after the first wave, and while *Model 5* may have generated some sort of suppression or destruction for a while, the operation was out of context as it did not precede a Command North offensive, nor was it followed by an ILAF offensive to attack Syrian ground forces from the air.

The concept of large-scale air superiority operations aimed at destruction of Egyptian and Syrian front-line deployments of SAM batteries collapsed primarily due to an absence of context, due to lack of coordination with Israeli Defense Force actions and operations. Air superiority over the front line has never been an objective but a means to accomplish an objective. Air defense did not threaten forces along a front line. Attacking a repairable integrated air defense system all along the front line without a context could have been neither a failure nor a success, but was a waste of effort.

The ILAF changed tactics to attacking smaller sectors – initially the Port Said deployment of SAM batteries – but again aimed at destruction, and again the ILAF action against Egyptian air defense units was not in the context of Command South offensives or calls for support.

Israeli Defense Force pressure finally forced the ILAF to accept that air superiority was not an objective but a means to enable air support. If AGM-45 missiles, chaff, and jamming, or even artillery fire aimed at adjacent SAM batteries, could secure an air support mission through local suppression of enemy air defenses for a short while, then actual destruction of the air defense system was not needed, primarily because the enemy's air defense forces did not threaten friendly ground forces.

Actual losses for Egyptian and Syrian air defense units are still unknown. The ILAF commander claimed in 1974 that 45 out of 62 Egyptian front-line SAM batteries had been destroyed by the end of the war, but that number included SAM batteries that had been destroyed or overrun by Israeli ground forces. The following year, ILAF research concluded that 35 SAM batteries had been suppressed from the air for 24–48 hours, including more than 20 that had been destroyed, slightly more than 10 percent of the estimated Egyptian and Syrian air defense prewar order of battle. In a 2013 statement commemorating 40 years since the war, the

Egypt's Qutamiya air base under ILAF Squadron 107 attack from 0810hrs on October 17, with red arrows pointing at hits, blue arrows at misses, and the northern arrow at the silhouette of a disengaging Kurnass. It is a typical image for an ILAF air base attack mission from the October 1973 War that did not produce the unambiguous destruction of aircraft photos acquired during similar missions from the June 1967 War, primarily due to Egypt and Syria learning lessons from the June 1967 War that included construction of some 700 and 200 shelters for aircraft, respectively, as well as construction of new air bases – such as Qutamiya – to deploy combat aircraft squadrons to more air bases. Consequently, even though the 1973 ILAF order of battle had been doubled from 1967, it was not able to attack all Egyptian and Syrian air bases within hours, as had been accomplished at the start of the June 1967 War. (AC)

ILAF support image from the June 1967 War showing Egyptian vehicles in Sinai – a few burning, some destroyed, many abandoned or damaged – after being attacked while retreating from the front line towards the Suez Canal. (AC)

ILAF claimed that 43 SAM batteries had been destroyed. Either way, the ILAF failed to accomplish the prewar objective of destroying the air defenses of Egypt and Syria.

ILAF air campaign to destroy Egyptian Air Force and Syrian Air Force

The ILAF air campaign against the Egyptian and Syrian air forces has been presented as successful, with advocates claiming that the ILAF committed to the task only some 700 sorties, supposedly suppressing Egyptian and Syrian air bases for the loss of only six aircraft.[69]

However, the ILAF's prewar plans aimed at destruction of the Egyptian Air Force and Syrian Air Force. Moreover, the ILAF's prewar presentation of plans to the Israeli Defense Minister yielded expectations that it would destroy the air forces of Egypt and Syria.

Though the Egyptian and Syrian air forces were considered to pose a relatively lower threat to Israel than other branches of the Egyptian and Syrian armed forces, the Israeli Defense Minister set Israel's armed forces an objective to win the war through destruction of the enemy, so ILAF plans to destroy their enemies' air forces were viewed as contributing to the overall goal rather than having a direct impact upon the battlefield, especially since the ILAF's prewar plans emphasized priority to attacking MiG-21 bases.

The ILAF did not destroy a single Egyptian or Syrian air base and fell short of prewar plans and expectations. The air forces of Egypt and Syria ended the war battered but functioning – the same as the ILAF – and the number of Egyptian and Syrian combat aircraft sorties flown during the closing days of the conflict were on a par with those during the opening days of the war.

ILAF air campaign to support the Israeli Defense Force

Egypt and Syria fielded 15 divisions. Iraq supported Syria with more than a division. Jordan and Morocco added a brigade each. With every division having more than 2,000 vehicles, there were more than 30,000 vehicles along the front lines, including more than 2,000 tanks and 2,000 pieces of artillery. Overall, there were tens of thousands of targets along the front lines, with tanks as the primary targets.

The ILAF recorded 5,142 support sorties – 46 percent of its counted combat aircraft sorties during the war – so support was its main effort during the October 1973 War, yet the term support is somewhat deceptive. There was no direct ILAF support for Israeli ground forces in the October 1973 War. Until the June 1967 War, the ILAF fielded Forward Air Controllers at brigade level who communicated directly with the supporting pilots. After the June 1967 War, the ILAF discarded brigade-level Forward Air Controllers , so during the October 1973 War ILAF pilots tasked to attack along the front line were in communication with an Israeli Defense Force command level Air Liaison Officer if the mission was support, or with the attack controller at the ILAF Regional Control Unit if the mission was an attack somewhere along the front line.

69 Elsewhere in this text the numbers of some 550 sorties and eight losses are presented to sum up ILAF's air campaign against Egyptian and Syrian bases. These are indeed the correct numbers. The number of 700 sorties is an ILAF count that includes sorties flown against Egyptian and Syrian bases as well as sorties flown against Egyptian and Syrian radar stations.

Close air support was therefore rarely accomplished, and Israeli field commanders often expressed frustration that ILAF support was not on time, not in place, and not on target. Again, it seems as though the Israeli Defense Force was giving the ILAF a free hand to attack along the front lines, bearing in mind the Israeli objective to win the war through destruction of the enemy; from the Israeli Defense Force's perspective, all that the ILAF could destroy along the front lines, on top of support to Israeli forces engaged in actual fighting, would get them closer to accomplishment of the Israeli government-set objective.

Hence, Israel invested some 50 percent of its prewar defense budget in the ILAF with a view to it generating mass destruction of targets along the front lines. Yet at the start of the war, ILAF stocks included only 214 precision air-to-ground weapons – AGM-12s, AGM-62s, and GBU-8s – so even if every such precision munition had hit a target, the overall impact would have been the destruction of only 200 out of more than 30,000 targets, an impact that would have been hardly noticed.

Most ILAF attack sorties over the front lines dropped bombs with a low statistical hit rate, and many of the bombs were delivered in loft profile, which further compromised accuracy, so the ILAF's share in destruction of meaningful targets along the front lines was probably far less than 50 percent and its share in destruction of tanks was negligible.[70]

At the start of the war, the ILAF failed to harass Egyptian crossing points and Syrian penetration paths. During the war, although the ILAF implemented lessons and improved, there was no mass destruction from the air of Egyptian and Syrian targets on the front lines, as may have been expected before the war. Towards the end of the war, even heavy and massive bombings of specific areas such as Hermon in the north or Missouri in the south did not collapse the enemy forces within the bombed compartments.[71]

ILAF air-to-air campaign

There was no independent air-to-air campaign during the October 1973 War. The ILAF attempted to draw the air forces of Egypt and Syria into the air-to-air arena, especially when attacking radar stations along Egypt's coastline and rear targets in Syria, when the ILAF positioned patrols mostly over the Mediterranean Sea and Red Sea to ambush Egyptian and

70 A relevant yardstick is comparison with Israeli Defense Force losses attributed to the Egyptian and Syrian air forces: the ILAF counted 1,351 Egyptian and Syrian offensive combat aircraft sorties over the front lines, the Israeli Defense Force reporting 265 casualties in air raids – possibly including friendly fire incidents – plus the loss of nine tanks and 24 vehicles.

71 Command North recaptured Hermon in heavy fighting with many casualties. Command South was unable to take Missouri, regardless of the ILAF bombings.

Towards the end of the war, the Egyptian Air Force committed to combat L-29 armed trainers that operated out of Bilbeis, an air base that the ILAF did not attack during the October 1973 War. The ILAF interpreted the commitment to combat of the L-29 armed trainers as a signal that Egypt's air force was in dire straits, reporting on October 22 that nine L-29s had been shot down. However, the final ILAF count was two L-29s shot down as air-to-air kills and two lost to AAA, with six further L-29 claims in doubt. These Nesher sight camera frames include the tracking of an L-29 tightly turning to starboard in the left frame and firing at the L-29 in the second frame (blurred due to firing, as well as presenting the black wedge at the top left corner that indicated firing), but the L-29 flew on, as shown in the third frame with Lake Bitter in the background. The Nesher fired again over what looks like a runway – perhaps Fayid – as captured in the fourth frame, but again the L-29 flew on, seemingly unharmed. The ILAF attributed one L-29 air-to-air kill to a Shafrir 2 launched by a Squadron 101 Nesher, while a second L-29 air-to-air kill was credited to Squadron 144 after an L-29 reportedly crashed while being chased by a Squadron 144 Nesher. (AC)

The ILAF Squadron 144 commander and the Israeli Defense Force Ground Liaison Officer attached to Squadron 144 brief the squadron's personnel at the end of a fighting day. The Israel Defense Force assigned an officer – mostly in charge of emphasizing the bomb line to avoid friendly fire incidents – to each squadron. The ILAF did not assign Forward Air Controllers to Israeli Defense Force brigades. Israel's aspiration and policy prior to the war had been painted on the Nesher's external fuel tank below the Squadron 144 commander's shoes: WE WANT PEACE. (AC)

Syrian interceptors. The ILAF's advantage in air-to-air encounters had been demonstrated before hostilities began, so the Egyptian and Syrian air forces preferred to avoid pure aerial combat. Most air combat was triggered during the ILAF campaign against targets to the rear of the front lines or during the Egyptian and Syrian air forces' campaign to support their ground forces across the front lines.

The initial ILAF air-to-air report from October 29 claimed 332 Egyptian and Syrian losses in air combats, compared to 17 Israeli losses, a 19.5-to-one kills-to-loss ratio, which was a very good ratio for the Israelis. The current official ILAF claim is 277 kills versus only five losses to enemy aircraft in air-to-air missions, resulting in a vastly upgraded 55-to-one kills-to-loss ratio. Confused?[72]

	ILAF end-of-war report[73]	ILAF end-of-war report[74]
air-to-air sorties	ILAF 4,405	ILAF 3,813 vs Egyptian and Syrian 11,084
AIM-7	used 12, kills 5	kills 3
AIM-9D	used 119, kills 67	kills 51
AIM-9G	used 13, kills 7	kills 1.5
Shafrir 2	used 176, kills 97	kills 89
guns	kills 85	kills 95.5–100.5
Total	kills 332 vs losses 17[75]	kills 277 vs losses 16[76]
kills-to-loss	19.5-to-1	55-to-1

Air-to-air combat resulted in a definitive ILAF victory. Such a success was not a surprise, as the ILAF held a clear prewar edge in air-to-air combat, yet the ILAF had not planned to destroy the air forces of Egypt and Syria in an air-to-air campaign. Indeed, destruction of an air force in an air-to-air campaign seems to have been the least efficient strategy to accomplish such a task. The ILAF air base attack campaign that initiated the June 1967 War had destroyed some 75 percent of Egypt's combat aircraft within a few hours, while during the 19 days of the October 1973 War ILAF claimed destruction of less than a third of Egyptian combat aircraft in air-to-air combats.

72　The key words are "losses to enemy aircraft in air-to-air missions." If an ILAF aircraft was lost to enemy aircraft in aerial combat while flying an air base attack mission, then the ILAF referred to the loss in the air base attack losses, not in the air-to-air losses.

73　Figures from ILAF Operations Defense Chief Oded Erez report, October 29 1973. (ILGOV Defense Archive)

74　ILAF History postwar research.

75　The 17 losses included seven Mirages and five Kurnasses lost in aerial combat, plus three Mirages and two Kurnasses lost to AAA/SAMs while fighting in an aerial combat or while flying an air-to-air mission.

76　The 16 losses comprised seven attributed to enemy aircraft, eight attributed to AAA/SAMs while fighting enemy aircraft, and one attributed to technical malfunction. The Kurnass lost to a Nesher in an aerial combat has been excluded, the loss being referred to as a loss during an air base attack mission. Out of seven losses attributed to enemy aircraft, the ILAF has presented only five as air-to-air losses.

ILAF combat aircraft claims and losses						
	Total	Force/front [1]	Air-to-air [2]	Air-to-ground	Ground-to-air	Additional losses [3]
Ahit	53	north 24 south 29	north - south possibly 1	-	north 23-24 south 26-29	north 0-1 south 0-2
Kurnass	32	north 15 south 17	north 2-3 south 2-3	-	north 10-12 south 11-13	north 1-2 south 1-4
Mirage	12	north 6 south 5	north 0-6 south 2-5	-	north 0-4 south 0-2	north 0-1 south 0-3 (test 1)
Saar	6	north 3 south 3	north - south possibly 1	-	north 2 south 2-3	1 take off accident on mission to north
TOTAL	103	north 48 south 54	north 2-9 south 4-10	-	north 35-40 south 39-49	north 2-5 south 1-11 (test 1)
Hunter	9	EGAF 9 SYAF -	EGAF 3 SYAF -	EGAF 1 SYAF -	EGAF 4 SYAF -	EGAF 1 SYAF -
MiG-17	85	EGAF 56 SYAF 29	EGAF 33 SYAF 17	EGAF 2 SYAF 1	EGAF 21 SYAF 7	EGAF - SYAF 4
MiG-21	219	EGAF 134 SYAF 85	EGAF 98 SYAF 63	EGAF 9 SYAF 6	EGAF 9 SYAF 2	EGAF 18 SYAF 14
Mirage	5	EGAF 5 SYAF -	EGAF 4 SYAF -	EGAF - SYAF -	EGAF 1 SYAF -	EGAF - SYAF -
Su-7	52	EGAF 29 SYAF 23	EGAF 19 SYAF 10	EGAF - SYAF 1	EGAF 6 SYAF 9	EGAF 4 SYAF 3
Su-20	10	EGAF 4 SYAF 6	EGAF 4 SYAF 5	EGAF - SYAF -	EGAF - SYAF -	EGAF - SYAF 1
TOTAL	380	EGAF 237 SYAF 143 [4]	EGAF 161 SYAF 95 [5]	EGAF 12 SYAF 8	EGAF 41 SYAF 18	EGAF 23 SYAF 22 [6]

NOTES

[1] ILAF claims of EGAF and SYAF losses include air expeditionary forces based in Egypt and Syria.

[2] ILAF attributed aircraft lost in air combat to fire from the ground and other causes (technical, fuel and even bird strike).

[3] Including friendly fire, technical malfunctions, fuel starvation, bird strike, CFIT = Controlled Flight Into Terrain, accidents etc.

[4] Maximum combat aircraft loss ratio between ILAF and EGAF SYAF was therefore 1-to-3.7 but was probably more realisticly at around 1-to-3.

[5] Maximum combat aircraft air-to-air kill ratio was therefore between 1-to-43 and 1-to-13.

[6] As indicated in the text an overlap between ILAF air-air, ground-air and other claims is possible.

The final balance

The ILAF may not have produced images of victory as it did in the June 1967 War. The ILAF may not have performed as well as may have been expected from prewar investments and promises. Nevertheless, the ILAF shaped the October 1973 War. The ILAF drove Egypt and Syria to develop their air defenses into formidable forces, therefore diverting funding from offensive ground forces.

The ILAF triggered the transformation of the air forces of Egypt and Syria into defensive-biased arms with heavy investment in shelters and smaller-scale offensive operations than what might have been expected from air arms fielding hundreds of combat aircraft. The ILAF also forced Egypt and Syria to modify Nasser's Phase 3 into a limited war with scaled-down objectives. The ILAF may have been the crucial factor behind Jordan's decision to avoid opening a third front.[77]

The ILAF in being – on top of its actual operations – was instrumental in Israel's victory in a war that would eventually realize the prewar Israeli objective of trading Sinai for peace.

77 Emphasizing the ILAF's impact upon the conduct of the war is its count of 6,674 offensive combat aircraft sorties and 3,813 defensive combat aircraft sorties, versus 1,351 Egyptian and Syrian offensive combat aircraft sorties and 11,084 Egyptian and Syrian defensive combat aircraft sorties.

BIBLIOGRAPHY

Aloni, Shlomo, *Ghosts of Atonement – Israeli F-4 Phantom Operations During the Yom Kippur War*, Schiffer Publishing, Atglen, Pennsylvania (2015)

Aloni, Shlomo, *Israeli A-4 Skyhawk Units in Combat*, Osprey Combat Aircraft 81, Osprey, Oxford (2009)

Aloni, Shlomo, *Israeli F-4 Phantom II Aces*, Osprey Aircraft of the Aces 60, Osprey, Oxford (2004)

Aloni, Shlomo, *Israeli Mirage and Nesher Aces*, Osprey Aircraft of the Aces 59, Osprey, Oxford (2004)

Aloni, Shlomo, *Six-Day War 1967: Operation Focus and the 12 hours that changed the Middle East*, Osprey Air Campaign 10, Osprey, Oxford (2019)

Cooper, Tom *et al.*, *Arab MiGs Volume 1–6*, Harpia Publishing, Austria (2009–15)

Cooper, Tom and Emran, Abdallah, *1973: The First Nuclear War: Crucial Air Battles of the October 1973 Arab-Israeli War*, Helion Middle East @ War 19, Helion, Warwick (2019)

Even-Epstein, Giora, *Hawkeye: The Enthralling Autobiography of the Top-Scoring Israel Air Force Ace of Aces*, Grub Street, London (2020)

Gordon, Yefim and Komissarov, Dmitriy, *Soviet and Russian Military Aircraft in the Middle East*, Hikoki Publications, Manchester (2013)

Nicolle, David, *Arab MiG-19 and MiG-21 Units in Combat*, Osprey Combat Aircraft 44, Osprey, Oxford (2004)

Nordeen, Lon and Nicolle, David, *Phoenix over the Nile: A History of Egyptian Air Power 1932–1994*, Smithsonian Institution Press, Washington DC (1996)

Shazly, Saad, *The Crossing of the Suez*, American Mideast Research, San Francisco (1980)

Spector, Iftach, *Loud and Clear*, Zenith Press, Minneapolis (2009)

Romm, Giora, *Solitary: The Crash, Captivity and Comeback of an Ace Fighter Pilot*, Black Irish Entertainment LLC, New York (2014)

United States Government Printing Office Foreign Relations of the United States, 1969–1976 Volume XXV, *Arab-Israeli Crisis and War, 1973* (2011)

INDEX